The Ultimate *G...* to
Cou... m
An *...cy*

The 50+ Best Places to Eat It

A Home-Curing Handbook

Old-Fashioned Recipes

Where to Order

by
Norman G. Marriott, Ph.D.
and
Herbert W. Ockerman, Ph.D.

Edited by Deborah Garrison Lowery

Marriott and Ockerman

The Ultimate Guide to
Country Ham
An American Delicacy

by
Norman G. Marriott, Ph.D.
and
Herbert W. Ockerman, Ph.D.

Edited by Deborah Garrison Lowery

The Ultimate Guide to Country Ham, © 2004,
Norman G. Marriott and Herbert W. Ockermann

Published by Brightside Press; Radford, Virginia
www. brightsidepress.com
brightside@nrvdc.org
540-633-6747

ISBN 1-888813-12-1

DEDICATION

To our dear friends, Vern and Ruth Cahill, who have provided us friendship and very enjoyable meals during the past.

TABLE OF CONTENTS

FORWARD

Country ham has been a part of my life as long as I can remember. As a boy I watched, and sometimes helped, Dad and the neighbors with the country ham ritual from hog-killing through curing. I always wanted to help mix the cure, but that was an honor belonging only to Mom or Dad. Of course, eating was, and still is, my favorite part of the whole process.

I remember watching the ham and bacon during aging and being anxious for the time when we could take it to the kitchen. In fact, I often tried to convince Mother that a country ham was ready to eat long before she agreed. I just couldn't wait to taste that rich flavor.

But it was years later when I truly began to appreciate the rich flavor of this southern tradition. As a meat science professor at Virginia Polytechnic Institute and State University in Blacksburg, Virginia, I learned about the real art and science involved with curing country ham. Experience and research taught me how to accentuate and increase the flavor of cured ham. Now, as a judge for many curing contests, I'm in "hog heaven" blending my personal love and professional expertise.

My partner and colleague, Herb Ockerman, joins me in relishing a childhood rich with country ham curing and dining traditions. As a meat science professor at Ohio State University, his research and love of country ham brought us together in this endeavor to preserve an age-old art and an appreciation for it.

Together, we teamed with freelance editor Deborah Lowery, a nationally recognized journalist whose background includes an extensive article about country ham for _Southern Living_ magazine (October 1986), and a love of the rich, cured flavor. It was our goal to compile the most complete guide in existence on a subject dear to our hearts and palates.

We hope that whether you like the challenge of curing a ham in your own backyard or just want to know the best place to eat it, that you'll find this book an enjoyable reference that will keep you appreciating one of the last true American delicacies.

Norman G. Marriott, Ph.D.
with Herbert W. Ockerman, Ph.D.

I

The Country Ham Story: Folklore and Fact

"Country ham---it's the romance of it, it's our culture, it's the number one Southern tradition that everyone relates to."

----Willard Scott,
Delaplane, Virginia

Marriott and Ockerman

Chapter 1

FOUR CENTURIES OF FLAVOR AND TRADITION

The first taste of country ham can be an eye-opener. The flavor of the barn-red meat can be a shock if you expect it to taste like the paler pink hams in the grocery stores.

"It has a twang to it," admits second generation country ham producer Wallace Edwards, of S. Wallace Edwards & Sons in Surry, Virginia. "The best comparison might be the difference in mild and sharp cheese. Aged cheese has a stronger flavor."

Country ham, like cheese and wine, also is aged for flavor. The longer it's aged the finer the texture and the drier the meat. And the drier the meat, the more concentrated the flavor that mingles saltiness and unforgettable sharpness. Yet the dry look can fool you. Watch closely as a razor-sharp knife trims paper-thin slices from the ham and you'll see it seep a slight amount of moisture assuring its juiciness.

Though the curing process has changed little through the centuries, there are subtle differences in curing, smoking, and aging that affect flavor. Because these variations tend to follow regional and state boundaries, debates over which is better are as easy to settle as disputes about religion, politics, or barbecue.

"I'd say most of the people I run into think a country ham is a country ham. They don't realize that there's a big variation," says Smith Broadbent III, third generation ham curer, associated with Broadbent B & B Foods in Cadiz, Kentucky.

But true lovers of country ham, especially in the traditional ham-curing states of Virginia, Kentucky, Tennessee, North Carolina, Georgia, and Missouri, know the choices: To smoke or not to smoke? To smoke with sassafras, hickory, or oak? To let it mold or not? To cure with salt and nitrate or add sugar and spices? To coat with black pepper, molasses, or sugar? To age it three months or a full year? To serve a pile of thin slices sandwiched in a biscuit or fry a thicker slice and drench it with red-eye gravy?

Secrets of the Flavor

What folks won't argue about is the fact that country ham has a flavor all its own. Even the tiniest piece of the mahogany meat is a rich and powerful burst of flavor. And that flavor doesn't come easily or cheaply. It takes time, temperature, humidity, and more time. But it's worth the wait.

"The flavor can be overpowering," admits Edwards. That's why the cured meat coveted by connoisseurs of great food traditionally is served with bland or sweet meats and accompaniments such as crabmeat, oysters, chicken, eggs, biscuits, sweet corn, or apples.

"There's nothing better than a good country ham with fried apples," says Edwards. "And around here you have to have the right biscuit. That means one that's so tender you have to be careful or it might break when you open it up."

Despite the pungency of cured ham, there are subtle flavor differences noted by discriminating palates. Sugar mixed into the salt cure counteracts the saltiness with a trace of sweetness. Hams swaddled in the scent of hickory smoke pick up the distinct hickory flavor. A pepper, sugar, or molasses outer coat on aged hams even adds a bit to the taste although the coatings are rinsed away before cooking. But, the most notable difference in flavor is determined by the length of aging time that can range from weeks to months. Longer aging means stronger flavor.

Unlike the pale pink hams in the supermarket meat counter that are injected with a pickle for preservation, country hams must first be hand-rubbed with dry salt and allowed to sit for weeks while the salt seeps into the meat and draws out moisture to preserve them. Then to develop the characteristic flavor, hams must be allowed to hang and age at warmer temperatures. Even with the use of advanced technology, this is a process that can't be rushed.

Cured hams labeled as "Smithfield hams" are among the longest aged and have the strongest flavor. They are cut with longer shanks than most country hams and aged no less than 180 days--by law. The average country ham ages about 90 days.

Another legal requirement of the Smithfield hams is that they must be produced within the city limits of Smithfield, Virginia. And according to Jim Groves of Smithfield Foods in Smithfield, no Smithfield ham leaves the premises without a traditional coating of black pepper.

The Curing Art

"A lot of the curing process is the art part and it's not something you can convey easily," says Wallace

Edwards. "For instance, my son and I can walk in a room of hams and from the aroma we can tell when it's right and when it's wrong."

The same "sniff test" is important for checking and aging ham to see if the salt penetrated the meat to cure it properly. It's the only way to test for a "bone sour" or rotten ham even in the most modernized plants today. An experienced worker will ram an ice pick deep into a ham then swing the pick up to his nose all with the flick of his wrist and in a matter of seconds. An "off" odor left on the pick detects a ham gone bad. Truly experienced workers actually can detect bad hams by thumping the pick handle against them.

These unique abilities, generally passed from one generation to the next, are the reason why most people who cure hams--whether it's in their backyard curing shed or in a commercial business--are simply carrying on a family tradition. And surprisingly, the process has changed little from 1608 when John Smith and the other settlers cured the first American hams.

Like the farmer who cures hams at home today, the earliest colonists were completely dependent on the proper weather conditions to cure their hams. They used wild or domesticated hogs, salt from evaporated seawater or from Indian tribes who mined salt, and continually stoked hardwood fires to preserve their hams with a process that took about one year.

They began in early winter while the weather was cold enough to keep the meat from spoiling. First they rubbed saltpeter (potassium nitrate or sodium nitrate), and then salt onto the surface of the meat. Sometimes they rubbed sugar or brown sugar onto the hams for extra flavor. Hams were laid in a tub of salt, and topped with more salt. More salt was added after five to seven days to help make sure the salt penetrated the meat.

About four to six weeks later in late winter the salted hams were washed and hung in a smokehouse. The rising temperatures and falling humidity during this period allowed the salt penetration to equalize throughout the entire ham. (Even today, this part of the curing process is called "equalization.") Then in the warmer days of spring, the hams were sometimes smoked for extra flavor.

During the drying and smoking process the hams shrunk and lost enough moisture to protect them from summer heat. After smoking, hickory ash or black pepper was often rubbed onto the surface of the hams to ward off insects. Then the aging process took place during the warmer summer months to develop the characteristic mellow flavor.

Country ham producers today follow the same salting-equalization-aging process. Some continue to use the temperature and humidity provided by Mother Nature. Others use temperature- and humidity-controlled environments that allow them to simulate the same seasonal changes. The advantage of the environmentally controlled rooms is that it allows producers to have hams in all stages at all times of the year. But, the process still is the same for true country hams.

The definition of country ham has sparked controversy over the years, especially when processes using salt brines were developed for quick-cure hams. At one time, any ham cured in the country, meaning outside the city limits, could be labeled as a country ham.

Today, the United States Department of Agriculture says that a true country ham is cured with a dry salt cure, loses at least 18% of its original weight in curing, and contains a minimum of 4% salt.

Even though buying a country ham is as easy as phoning in a mail-order, there are plenty of folks who don't mind taking the trouble and time to cure their own. (For home-curing instructions see Chapter 5).

Pink "Tiny" Guier, a farmer in Cadiz, Kentucky, still cures over 100 hams a year in his backyard smokehouse. "I just like to do it, I guess," he says. Tiny can't remember when he didn't know how to cure hams. As a boy, he helped and learned from his dad who passed down ham curing knowledge traced back at least eight generations.

The American Roots of Country Ham

Though other cultures around the world have dry-cured ham for centuries, there is no doubt that the American ham-curing process has its roots in Virginia. The first hams were cured in the Jamestown colony.

One story suggests that John Smith adopted the curing process for preserving game used by the Warascoyak Indians or another nearby tribe. Folks in Smithfield, Virginia, even claim that country ham, not the brave Pocahontas, spared Smith's life from Powhatan's wrath all because Smith held the secret recipe for Smithfield ham.

We do know that English colonists brought hogs with them to the new country. The hog population grew so quickly that the settlers moved the animals to an island on the James River near Smithfield where they ran wild and foraged on acorns and other nuts. John Smith aptly named it "Hog Isle." It's still called Hog Island today.

Because the port city of Smithfield saw its share of international trade, cured Virginia hams were shipped throughout the world. Even though hams have been cured for centuries in other countries, the distinct taste of hams from the area rose in demand. Many Europeans began to request Virginia hams or Smithfield hams.

Speculation is that the unique flavor came from the oily acorns, peanuts, hickory nuts, and beechnuts on which the hogs foraged, along with the hickory smoke used to season the hams. In fact, once the colonists began raising peanuts, hogs were often turned into the harvested fields and allowed to root for leftover nuts. Although hogs are not fed on peanuts today, some country ham customers believe hams from peanut-fed hogs are better than others.

Having a ham in the smokehouse still was a common practice in the early 1900's. The hams did not need refrigeration, so they were easy to store. Even after slicing a ham, the cut sides were often slathered in lard, pressed back together, and placed back in the cloth sack to hang.

Birth of a Business

By the end of the Revolutionary War, Virginia hams were in great demand. Sea captains traded hams for goods and offered them as gifts during their travels.

Smithfield, the Virginia port town named for Arthur Smith, a relative of John Smith's, became synonymous with country ham. Records show that hams from the area were exported routinely as early as 1783.

One of the first companies to produce country ham in commercial quantities was Todd's Packing House in Smithfield. Officially established in 1800 by Bermudian sea captain Mallory Todd, sales have been traced to 1779, making it the oldest firm to be founded in Virginia.

Later named the E.M. Todd Company, it was eventually sold to the Armistead Churchill Young family who operated it from Richmond for three generations. Then, in 1998 the company was acquired by The Smithfield Companies and returned to Smithfield, 220 years after Mallory Todd's first recorded sale.

Sales receipts show that Todd's hams were popular among royalty. During Queen Victoria's reign, his hams were served at Windsor Castle, a tradition that continues today. Country ham still is on the menu for Queen Elizabeth II and her family.

During the colonial period, country ham biscuits were served at most lavish parties and noted events. Two centuries later, General Pershing served country ham at an important banquet in Paris after World War I. It was on the menu again in Berlin at a four-power dinner celebrating the end of World War II.

In the early 1930's the Barter Theater in Abington, Virginia, accepted country hams in exchange for tickets to plays. The tradition started when many people could afford to see the plays only by trading food for admission. The hams allowed the theater actors and actresses to be fed as partial payment for their performance. Theater owner Robert Porterfield even presented a country ham as part of the Barter Award, which was given to the best performer of the year. And he sometimes paid royalties with country hams. In keeping with tradition, the Barter Theater accepts country hams today as trade for tickets of equal value.

One aspect of history common to almost all country ham producers is that the ham flavor itself birthed the business. Generally, a farmer who cured hams for his family or to sell a few on the side responded to the demand and started a business that often has been passed down through the generations. Business for S. Wallace Edwards & Sons began when ferry captain Wallace Edwards sold country ham sandwiches to the patrons crossing the James River. "He cured 55 hams his first year in 1926," explains his son, S. Wallace Edwards, Jr. "Mother cooked them, he sliced them. Then my father sold them to people crossing the river. Ferry customers began to request hams, so his business actually started as mail-order."

The stories are similar across the ham-curing states. A farmer cured hams for his family, shared them or sold them to friends and neighbors, then increased the number of hams he cured to meet the growing demand.

Country Ham's Comeback

The demand for country ham has never waned among those that grew up relishing the flavor. But as people moved away from the country and cities grew, generations were born who never knew about or tasted country ham.

Grocery sales increased when stores stocked packaged goods that responded to the consumer desire for convenience and speed cooking. Meals in the early 1980's were eat-and-run as families spent more time away from home and less time in the kitchen. Soaking, simmering, then baking a traditional country ham was out of the question for the average person.

It wasn't long before the country ham industry responded to consumer demand. By the mid-1980's country hams were sold pre-cooked, boneless, and even pressed into loaves for deli-style slicing.

But the real comeback to country ham started when noted chefs recognized it as a powerful flavor ingredient. Country ham showed up in upscale dishes in the prestigious Culinary Olympics where chefs compete with their creations in the international competition. Award-winning chefs like Marcel Desaulniers of The Trellis in Williamsburg, Virginia, and Frank Stitt, of Highlands Bar and Grill, in Birmingham, Alabama, began incorporating the regional flavor into their own signature recipes.

Today, the return to flavor and to regional food treasures has turned attention back to country ham. Consumers can savor the flavor without the work by ordering small-sized cooked portions. Those that demand the best, including stars like Clint Eastwood, are regulars on the mail-order customer lists.

But the old-time lovers of country ham are alive and well and continuing the tradition. Wallace Edwards tells about one family that has made an annual trek to his Surry smokehouse for three generations to buy their holiday ham.

In Cadiz, Kentucky, Tiny Guier sells some of his hams, but as a home business operator he cannot ship them. That doesn't bother one of his regular customers from Valdosta, Georgia. "He comes every year all the way from Georgia," says Tiny. "He told me that it's 559 miles from his driveway to mine. But he just keeps on coming."

CURED HAMS AROUND THE WORLD

TYPE HAM: COUNTRY OF ORIGIN; DESCRIPTION

Prosciutto or Parma: Italy (Parma region). Dry-cured, unsmoked, Aged 7 to 24 months. Eaten uncooked.

Katenschinken: Germany (Westphalian region). Cured with dry and immersion processes. Stored 4 to 9 weeks before aging. Aged 1 month in refrigeration. Smoked with juniper twigs & berries over beechwood fire for 1 week after aging.

Sauna: Finland. Similar to U.S. country ham

Serrano: Spain. Dry-cured 6-30 months. Unsmoked. Mold covering. Eaten uncooked.

Yunan or Jinhwa: China. Dry-cured with salt. Aged at least 6 months. Usually cooked.

Cumberland: England. Dry-cured with salt, potassium nitrate, and sugar for at least 1 month. Aged at least 2 months.

Jambon de Bayonne: France. cured with sea salt and aged 7-12 months. Often spiced with Espelette pepper.

Chapter 2

RIVALRY AND REGIONAL DIFFERENCES

It doesn't take an expert to identify the regional differences in dry-cured country hams. If it's long-cut, smoked, coated with black pepper, and has no trace of sugar in the cure, it must be from southeastern Virginia.

If it's hickory-smoked, pecan-colored, and cured with a bit of sugar, then it's likely from Western or Northern Kentucky or Western Tennessee. Light mahogany colored hams dry-cured without smoke are a trademark of mountainous Eastern Kentucky, Eastern Tennessee, and Western North Carolina.

Dig deeper into the differences and you can almost trace the cured ham to the county it came from. Some ham producers use a trademark hardwood for smoking like apple, maple, pecan, hickory, or even sassafras. Others season their salt cure with spices, dried honey, or molasses.

The regional variations in country hams were more distinct years ago than they are today now that the curing operations are more standardized. But loyalty to locally produced hams is as fierce as that for the region's barbecue or favorite football team.

The Smithfield Ham

The most famous of dry-cured hams is named for the city in which it's cured---Smithfield, Virginia.

25

According to law, a ham labeled as a "genuine Smithfield ham" must be produced within the city limits.

"The Smithfield hams have about 30% shrink from green (uncured) weight," explains Jim Groves of Smithfield Foods. "Country hams take only about 21% shrink. What we do is dry out these (Smithfield) hams more."

This extra drying by longer aging is what makes the Smithfield hams saltier than country hams cured for shorter periods of time. Visually a Smithfield ham (don't call it a "country" ham to a local!) is identified by its long shank and a coating of blue-green mold. The extra aging time produces the coat of mold.

Customers know to expect the mold, just as they expect to find a coating of black pepper beneath the mold. Although pepper doesn't contribute much to the flavor, the hams are coated in the spice for tradition's sake before they are smoked with a combination of hickory, oak, and apple woods.

Though any producer can produce a long shank, long-aged dry-cured ham that looks like the traditional Smithfield ham, they can't call it a "Smithfield" unless the process took place in you-know-where. Instead, they identify these Smithfield twins as longer-aged or long-cure hams.

Friendly Competition

For an art form that takes nearly a year to complete, it seems natural that the annual state fair is where producers and amateur ham curers would gather to decide who does it best.

At the **Virginia State Fair** in Richmond each fall (usually September and October) commercial producers and amateur ham curers (including a youth division) compete for the coveted Grand Champion ham award. During the past, the winning ham has received the honor of being presented to the governor on Governor's Day.

For more information about the Virginia State Fair Country Ham Competition write: **State Fair of Virginia, P.O. Box 26805, Richmond, VA 23261, or call 804-569-3200-http://statefair.com/**

Every August at the **Kentucky State Fair** in Louisville, cured ham competition between commercial ham producers continues in a big way and the public is invited. After the winner is announced the Grand Champion ham is auctioned for charity. The bidding takes place at the annual Kentucky Country Ham Breakfast sponsored by Kentucky Farm Bureau Federation on the second Thursday of the fair.

The breakfast is open to anyone with a ticket, and features Kentucky-produced center-cut country ham steaks with red-eye gravy, eggs, biscuits, butter, sorghum, and milk. The ham steaks are grilled by Kentucky ham producers for up to 1600 ticket holders. Bidding for the ham begins after the meal.

In 2003 the Grand Champion ham brought $250,000, the most ever bid since the contest began in 1964. Altogether, 40 years of Grand Champion hams have raised over $1,000,000 for worthy causes of the successful bidder's choice.

For tickets or more information write: **Kentucky Country Ham Breakfast, Kentucky Farm Bureau Federation, P.O. Box 20700, Louisville, KY 40250, or call 502-495-5106.**

For more information about other state fair ham competitions, contact the state fair office of individual states.

What Makes A Winning Ham?

Hams from producers and home-curers alike are judged at fairs and festivals through the ham-producing states. Categories may be divided into smoked, non-smoked, long cut, and short cut. Judges assign points for the following criteria to determine the winning ham.

Trim: How and where the shank end of the bone is cut, beveled cut of the leg, and how the top (large) part of the ham is trimmed.

Color: Reddish pink and uniform color throughout

Fat to lean ratio: Acceptable amount of muscle without excessive fat layer on the exterior surface and in the seams (between muscles)

Flavor: Mellow, aged flavor with a cured aroma when cooked

Saltiness: Salty taste not overpowering when cooked

<u>Tenderness:</u> Determined by the amount of force required when the ham is cut

Where to Celebrate Country Ham

Country ham is cause for some big celebrations around the region. In Smithfield, North Carolina, the annual **Ham and Yam Festival** started in 1983 with a challenge from North Carolina to Virginia. The two Smithfields decided to have a showdown to determine who cured a better ham and to provide year-long bragging rights for the winner. Supposedly Smithfield, North Carolina, won the uncooked ham competition that year and Smithfield, Virginia exhibited the champion cooked ham.

Although a country ham competition is no longer part of the festival, the town of Smithfield, North Carolina, continues with the annual celebration in honor of the farmers of the area. Every third weekend in April the Kiwanis club sells country hams, the Downtown Smithfield Development Corporation sponsors a country ham raffle, and the competitions include a ham cooking contest and children's yam decorating contest. Sugar-sprinkled "yam fries" are a favorite tradition.

For more information about the Ham and Yam Festival, write: **Ham and Yam Festival, Smithfield Downtown Development Corporation, P.O. Box 761, Smithfield, N.C. 27577, or call, 919-934-0887.**

In the tiny town of Cadiz, Kentucky, the second week of October means a party---all on account of country ham. The town swells to a crowd of 30,000 people who drop by just for the **Trigg County Country Ham Festival**. The weekend-long celebration of country ham is kicked off with a buffet ham breakfast at Lake Barkley State Resort Park in Cadiz.

During the festival weekend, Broadbent B&B Foods, the local country ham producer, bakes a 10-1/2-foot country ham biscuit and sells pieces of it to donate to charity. The whopper of a ham biscuit was first baked in a specially designed oven in 1986 where Guinness Book of World Records dubbed it "the World's Largest Country Ham Biscuit". However, Smithfield Foods broke the record in 2003 with a ham biscuit that weighed 2000 pounds. It was made to feed 1752 people-the year of Smithfield, Virginia's charter.

Festivities for the weekend include a parade, greased pig contest, kiss-the-pig contest, a home-cured country ham competition, and daily country ham giveaways.

For more information write: **Trigg County Ham Festival, Trigg County Tourist Commission and Cadiz Chamber of Commerce, 22 Main Street, Cadiz, Kentucky 42211, or call 270-522-3892.**

Chapter 3

THE 50+ BEST PLACES
TO EAT COUNTRY HAM

If you want to know the real story of country ham, then you need to go to the places where the flavor has been served and savored for decades--the restaurants, the diners, and the hard-to-find cafes where all the locals and in-the-know visitors go to get some good country ham. These are familiar haunts where the hunters head for an early morning breakfast, farmers show up for the noon meal, business travelers plan their routes around them, and tourists visit again and again. Most are steeped in family history, just like the companies that produce hams. All have a story to share; many cure the hams they serve, or did at one time.

Some of the diners and cafes known for serving the best country ham aren't on the map. Many of them don't even advertise. In fact, your best bet for finding them might be to stop and ask directions when you get in town.

Then there are the dignified inns featuring southern cuisine and a bit more sophistication. They're easier to find, but their stories are just as colorful as the backwoods gems.

And now, even upscale five-star restaurants

serve up a taste of the rich-flavored regional delicacy in contemporary dishes that have customers coming back for more.   Though they often blend a new style of cooking with the old country ham favorite, you can still find history, lore, and a legacy of country ham.

The following restaurants have made country ham a regular part of their menu. Some serve it at breakfast only, others three times daily, still others as a surprise ingredient in a recipe created by the chef that day. Check for serving hours and the preferred method of payment; some accept cash only. It's also a good idea to make reservations, if possible. Many of the restaurants report waits of up to 3 hours for drop-in guests.

ALABAMA

Uncle Mort's Restaurant, Jasper
9145 Highway 78
205-483-7614
Specialty: fried ham on a country-style menu
Note of interest: The restaurant also sells whole hickory-smoked cured hams, but has no mail-order sales.

GEORGIA

The Dillard House Restaurant, Dillard
768 Franklin Street
706-746-5348 or 800-541-0671
Specialty: fried ham served daily and honey-baked whole country hams served at Thanksgiving and Christmas meals on a Southern country-style menu

Note of interest: Whole country hams are for sale on-site and by mail-order.

Swamp Guinea, Hartwell
76 Rowland Road
706-376-5105
Specialty: all-you-can-eat fried ham on family-style menu
Note of interest: The restaurant is located on popular Lake Hartwell. A boat dock and pier leading to the restaurant accommodate customers who arrive by boat.

KENTUCKY

KENTUCKY STATE RESORT PARKS

Though the menus vary a bit at the 17 resort parks, you can expect to find fried ham with red-eye gravy for breakfast, center-cut country ham steaks for dinner, and creamy country ham dressing almost any time. Slices of simmered, baked whole ham are served on holidays such as Mother's Day and Easter. At Lake Barkley State Park in Cadiz, a country ham breakfast buffet kicks off the Trigg County Ham Festival every second weekend of October.

For directions and more detailed information about individual parks, call
1-800-255 PARK (7275) or check the Kentucky State Park website:
http://www.kystateparks.com/

East Kentucky:

Barren River Lake State Resort Park, Lucas
270-646-2151

Blue Licks Battlefield State Resort Park, Mt. Olivet
859-289-5507

Buckhorn Lake State Resort Park, Buckhorn
606-398-7510

Carter Caves State Resort Park, Olive Hill
606-286-4411

Cumberland Falls State Resort Park, Corbin
606-528-4121

Dale Hollow Lake State Resort Park, Bow
270-433-7431

General Butler State Resort Park, Carrollton
502-732-4384

Greenbo Lake State Resort Park, Greenup
606-473-7324

Jenny Wiley State Resort Park, Prestonsburg
606-886-2711

Lake Cumberland State Resort Park, Jamestown
270-343-3111

Natural Bridge State Resort Park, Slade
606-663-2214

Pine Mountain State Resort Park, Pineville
606-337-3077

West Kentucky:

Kenlake State Resort Park, Hardin
270-474-2211 or 800-325-0143

Kentucky Dam Village State Resort Park, Gilbertsville
502-732-4384

Lake Barkley State Resort Park, Cadiz
270-924-1131

Pennyrile Forest State Resort Park, Dawson Springs
270-797-3421

Rough River Dam State Park, Falls of Rough
270-257-2311

Beaumont Inn, Harrodsburg
638 Beaumont Inn Drive
859-734-3381 or 800-352-3992/ reservations suggested
http://www.beaumontinn.com
Specialty: 2-year old Kentucky cured hams on a menu
featuring Kentucky and southern regional foods in traditional and contemporary recipes

Note of Interest: The historic inn, once a college, is run by the Dedman family.

Oak Room at the Seelbach Hilton, Louisville
500 4th Avenue
502-585-9292/reservations suggested
Specialty: southern regional inspired menu with signature dishes of country ham-stuffed chicken with bourbon sauce; country ham-portaebello-artichoke ravioli; and fresh water shrimp with country ham hush puppy tempura & ginger chow chow
Note of interest: The restaurant, built in 1907 as a "gentlemen's only" billiards room, is Kentucky's only 5-diamond restaurant.

Claudia Sanders Dinner House, Shelbyville
3202 Shelbyville Road
502-633-5600
Specialty: fried and simmered country ham on a country-style menu
Note of Interest: This 30-year-old restaurant was started by Colonel Sanders and his wife after Sanders sold Kentucky Fried Chicken. The building was once the KFC office headquarters and warehouse.

MISSOURI

Stephenson's Old Apple Farm Restaurant,
Kansas City
(Rick Stephenson)
16401 East 40 Highway
816-373-5400/will take reservations
Specialty: fried ham with wine & honey sauce on a country-fine dining menu
Note of Interest: Family owned since 1946, the restaurant uses products from Stephenson family orchard.

Lambert's Cafe
Ozark: 1800 West Highway J
*   417-581-7655*
Sikeston: 2515 East Malone
*   573-471-4261*
Specialty: skillet-fried ham
Note of interest: It's famous for its "throwed rolls." Says the manager, "When you sit down, a guy comes from the kitchen pushing a cart and yelling, 'hot rolls!' If you want one you just stick up your hand and he'll throw you one."

Nic Nac Cafe, California
Highway 50 West
573-796-2821
Specialty: fried ham on a family dining menu
Note of interest: The cafe has been owned by the same family for more than 20 years; it's the only family dining restaurant in town.

Westphalia Inn Restaurant, Westphalia
106 West Main Street
573-455-9991/reservations suggested; open only Fri,
Sat, & Sun
Specialty: skillet-fried ham served with fried chicken on a family-style all-you-can-eat menu that has been the same for 40 years
Note of interest: The restaurant is located in an inn built in 1928; customers enjoy the owner's antique collection in the lobby. The owners live in renovated upper floors of the hotel.

NORTH CAROLINA

Daniel Boone Inn, Boone
130 Hardin Street (near Appalachian State University
campus)
828-264-8657
Specialty: fried ham and biscuits served with family-style meal
Note of interest: The original part of the building was Boone's first hospital. When the restaurant, now in business for 40 years, expanded and enclosed a porch, they built around an unusual tree, an oak and maple that grew together sharing the same trunk. The oak, which once protruded from the second floor window, died. But the maple, which grows out of the first floor window, is still an attraction.

Shatley Springs Inn, Crumpler
Highway 16, 407 Shatley Springs Road   (8 miles south
of VA/NC state line)
336-982-2236/reservations suggested, no reservations
on Saturdays and Sundays
Specialty: fried ham and country ham biscuits on family-style menu
Note of interest: Cabins and a tea room were built in the 1920's near the spring waters known for their healing properties; the present restaurant is in the old tea room. Be prepared for up to a 3-hour wait for weekend meals. Entertainment includes gospel, country, and bluegrass musicians who work for gratuities and an overnight stay in a cabin. Look for keyboardist, singer, and accordion player, Peggy, who sings for special occasions, and loves to entertain children.

Smoky Mountain Barbecue, West Jefferson
1008 South Jefferson
336-246-6818
Specialty: old fashion country ham, whole hog barbecue, pig pickins
Note of interest: "We will sell no swine until its time."

The Country House, Elk Park
Highway 19E
828-733-4027
Specialty: fried ham; also known for plate-sized biscuits at breakfast
Note of interest: The 20-year-old restaurant is a local hangout where folks feel at home. "We're different," says owner Peggy Burleson. "People who come here

sometimes get their own coffee and clean their own tables if we're busy."

Greenfield Restaurant, West Jefferson
1795 Mount Jefferson Road
336-246-2900
Specialty: fried ham and ham biscuits served 3 times a day on a country-style menu
Note of interest: The 40-year-old restaurant has a beautiful view of North Carolina rural countryside.

Blue Point Restaurant, Duck
in the Waterfront shop along N.C. Highway 12
252-261-8090/reservations required
Specialty: country ham added to pasta, soup, omelets and various other menu selections in seasonal upscale Southern regional cuisine; ham often served as a garnish
Note of interest: This restaurant is on the sound and features a retro-50's style diner decor.

TENNESSEE

Shirley's Restaurant, Hampton
3266 Highway 321
423-768-2092
Specialty: fried ham served family-style on choice of menus: meat-and-three vegetables or the "works" which includes another specialty, cornbread salad

Note of Interest: The restaurant is in a former gas station building deep in the Smoky Mountains, and is closed during winter.

Miss Mary Bobo's Boarding House Restaurant, Lynchburg
925 Main Street
931-759-7394/reservations required, serves breakfast and lunch only
Specialty: baked ham is served often on a changing old-fashioned family-style menu and everyday in December when Christmas dinner is served daily
Note of Interest: Lynchburg is the home of Jack Daniels Distillery, the oldest registered distillery in the U.S. Lynne Tolley, proprietress of the inn, is the great-grand niece of Jack Daniels. "We cook with Jack Daniels every day," she says.

Applewood Farmhouse Restaurant, Sevierville
240 Apple Valley Road
865-428-1222
Specialty: center-cut fried slices with red-eye gravy and country ham biscuits; known for apple fritters and apple butter served at each table when guests are seated for a family-style meal
Note of interest: The restaurant is in an old farmhouse. The original farmhouse owner runs the attached Apple Barn, Cider Mill, and General Store where you can browse the store and feed ducks at a nearby pond while you wait.

VIRGINIA

Lake View Motel & Restaurant, Fancy Gap
Jct 52 & Blue Ridge Parkway
276-728-7841
Specialty: Country ham, steaks, and snacks
Note of interest: It's located close to Blue Ridge Parkway and I-77.

Martha Washington Inn, Abingdon
150 West Main Street
276-628-3161/dinner reservations suggested
Specialty: fried ham for breakfast, available on request for dinner; whole-cooked sliced ham usually on Christmas Day buffet
Note of Interest: Country ham biscuits can be included in a picnic box lunch packed by the kitchen on request.

Mountain Top Motel & Restaurant, Fancy Gap
U.S. 52 & Blue Ridge Parkway
276-728-9414
Specialty: Country ham, steaks, and seafood
Note of interest: It's located close to Blue Ridge Parkway and I-77.

Indian Fields Tavern, Charles City
9220 John Tyler Memorial Highway
804-829-5004/reservations suggested

Specialty: serves country ham in contemporary regional cuisine in recipes such as crab cakes over Smithfield ham & Sally Lunn bread or open-faced sandwich of Smithfield ham, Swiss cheese, & tomatoes on Sally Lunn bread

Note of interest: The restaurant is a 19th century restored farmhouse located about an hour's drive from Richmond.

The Homeplace, Catawba
4968 Catawba Valley Drive
540-384-7252

Specialty: country ham, roast beef, and fried chicken

Note of interest: Meals are served home style in an old farmhouse in the beautiful Catawba Valley.

Chickahominy House, Williamsburg
1211 Jamestown Road
757-229-4689

Specialty: known for country ham biscuits served all day; serves pan-browned ham slices for breakfast; also known for Brunswick stew, chicken & dumplings, and homemade pies

Note of interest: The thin, square biscuits served with country ham are a trademark of the Chickahominy House.

The Jefferson Restaurant, Williamsburg
1453 Richmond Road
757-229-2296

Specialty: Virginia ham, Virginia peanut soup, and baked stuffed pork chops

Note of interest: Since 1956, Harriett Petrell, the Matriarch, and now 4 generations of her family and her staff, have been serving local patrons and travelers.

The Trellis, Colonial Williamsburg
403 Duke of Gloucester Street
757-229-8610/reservations suggested

Specialty: changing contemporary regional cuisine menu features selections such as grilled cheese & scallops with zucchini & country ham; fennel, red pepper, & country ham soup; grilled chicken breast with peaches, black pepper, butter, & country ham

Note of interest: The restaurant serves the original "Death by Chocolate" dessert. Each serving weighs 1 pound, 2 ounces.

The Williamsburg Inn Restaurant,
Colonial Williamsburg
231 Francis Street
757-229-1000/reservations requested

Specialty: fried ham at breakfast; ham & biscuits at tea; lunch and dinner selections of smoked ham shank over black-eyed peas & wilted greens, oven-roasted ham with mustard, maple syrup, & cloves, pineapple bread pudding with ham slices & raisin sauce

Note of interest: Guests can enjoy a meal or tea with a costumed personality from the past including Thomas Jefferson, Martha Washington, and Governor Spotswood.

Smithfield Inn, Smithfield
112 Main Street
757-357-1752

Specialty: simmered and thinly sliced Smithfield ham is served as an accompaniment to many recipes; yeast rolls and sweet potato rolls stuffed with Smithfield ham served at both the fine dining inn restaurant and the more casual tavern at all times and often ordered "to go" by drop-in customers

Note of interest: The inn was built in 1752 as a stagecoach stop, then became licensed as a tavern in 1756. The English-style tavern is a traditional gathering place where newcomers meet the locals.

Smithfield Station, Smithfield
415 South Church Street
757-357-7700

Specialty: serves aged Smithfield ham only; famous for three specialties served daily-Tornadoes Christina (Smithfield ham & beef medallions with Bernaise sauce); Chicken Isle of Wight (rolled chicken breast with Smithfield ham, Swiss cheese, & peanuts topped with cream sauce); and Surf & Turf (Smithfield ham & two crab cakes).

Note of interest: Smithfield Station is a combination hotel, restaurant, and marina on the water in Smithfield's historic district.

Surrey House Restaurant, Surry
11865 Rolfe Highway
757-294-3389 or 800-200-4977

Specialty: baked, fried, and grilled ham served on country-style menu

Note of interest: The 1950's-style roadhouse has been in business since 1954.

Virginia Diner, Wakefield
Highway 460
757-899-3106

Specialty: Virginia country ham, pork barbecue, peanut soup, homemade biscuits, and southern grits

Note of interest: This diner started in a refurbished railroad car in 1929 that has since been replicated.

WASHINGTON, D.C.

Morrison Clark Inn
1015 L Street (corner of 11th Street and L Street)
202-898-1200/reservations suggested
Specialty: contemporary fine dining with a changing menu that includes country ham featured in selections such as country ham-cheddar souffle; Southern-style chopped salad with country ham-seasoned biscuits; and shrimp & artichoke tart with gruyere & country ham. At least one dish on every Sunday brunch menu features country ham.
Note of Interest: The Victorian dining room is located in an historic inn. In good weather, an outdoor enclosed courtyard is open for dining.

Cracker Barrel and Country Ham

"We've always served country ham," says Jennifer Presley, a Cracker Barrel representative. At any time of the day customers can order up fried ham, ham and biscuits, or a country ham sandwich on sourdough bread at any of the 400 Cracker Barrel restaurants located in 36 states.

Each of the restaurants sport a country store-style decor complete with a front porch and rocking chairs for waiting guests and a large fireplace in the dining area. To get to the dining area, customers weave through a store featuring old-fashioned candies and other country-style products. The store even sells cooked and uncooked country hams and country ham gift packs by mail (see list of mail-order sources, page 84).

To find out the location of a Cracker Barrel Restaurant call the company headquarters in Lebanon, Tennessee, at **615-444-5533.** Or, look up the website at *www.crackerbarrel.com* where you can request a free map of all Cracker Barrel locations. Most are located just off interstates.

II

The Home-Curing Handbook

"It's the continuity of our culture, the romance of a Southern tradition that everyone relates to that keeps me curing my own hams. In fact, I'll bet some of the ashes in my smokehouse are some of the same ones left by my grandfather when he started curing hams in 1914. I love the idea of that."

--- *Willard Scott*
Delaplane, Virginia

Marriott and Ockerman

Chapter 4

HOW TO GET STARTED

It's no accident that the boundaries of the traditional ham-curing states include Virginia, North Carolina, Kentucky, Tennessee, north Georgia, and Missouri. Home-cured hams, like commercially dry-cured hams, are dependent upon only three factors: temperature; time; and humidity. While commercial producers can simulate the ideal temperature and humidity for curing in any location, home curers are totally dependent upon the year-long weather conditions in their area.

Before you consider dry-curing a ham at home, call the local county extension office to find out if your area's weather makes it worth the effort.

Choose the Right Ham

The ideal ham comes from a healthy, fast-growing pig less than 6-1/2 months old with a high lean to fat ratio. If you don't butcher your own hogs, buy a USDA or state-inspected fresh ham from a local grocer, meat market, or meat processing firm.

Size: If you plan to cure more than one ham, try to select hams that are of similar size and shape. One way to do this is to select cuts or live hogs from a specific weight range. A hog that weights 225 to 265 pounds will yield uncured hams from 16 to 22 pounds.

Color: Start with a fresh ham with a grayish-pink to light red color. This color will vary from one muscle to another, but it should be fairly uniform throughout the ham. You'll also notice that the older the hog, the darker the color of the meat.

If you choose a ham that is too pale, it will not develop a bright cured color after curing. And, it's likely that the meat will turn an unattractive gray or green during the curing process.

Fat color is not as critical as lean meat color, but it's best to choose a ham with snow white fat.

Shape: The ham shape is an indicator of the ratio of lean to fat and bone. The best shaped ham is wide at the cut surface and has a minimum, but uniform, fat covering. The seam fat between the exposed muscles should be minimal and the exposed lean meat near the aitch (pelvis) bone should be plump and rounded.

Also check the middle portion (called the cushion) of the ham; a good indication of the meatiness of the ham is detected here. It should be plump, long, and wide. The shank on a heavily muscled ham will appear shorter because the muscle development extends down the shank and ends closer to the hock.

Marbling: Flakes of fat in the lean uncured meat, called marbling, are important for flavor and firmness. There should be a small amount of marbling. If the meat is too lean and soft, the ham will lose more moisture during the curing process and become tougher. Also look for open seams between the muscles where insects can enter.

Freshness: You can tell how fresh a ham is by the color of the lean muscle and fat. A dark, dry, or hard surface means the meat is not fresh. The fat on older hams is grayish rather than snow white.

Trim: It's important to trim just the right amount of fat from the ham. Too much fat will keep the cure from penetrating correctly and prevent the ham from losing moisture necessary for preservation. Trim the fat evenly over the ham, leaving about 1/4-inch of fat covering over the lean tissue. If lean meat is exposed, it will cause the areas to dry, harden, and discolor.

Temperature: It's important to start the curing process with a ham that is between 32°F and 40°F. A higher temperature may mean that bacteria have an opportunity to grow and spoil the ham. Lower temperatures will retard the salt penetration process and prevent preservation of the meat.

The Cure Ingredients

The ingredients used to cure ham include salt, sugar, nitrate, and nitrite. Each is used to preserve the meat or to develop color and flavor as it cures.

Salt: This is the only ingredient necessary for curing. It serves as a preservative and flavor enhancer by helping the muscle absorb sugar, which counteracts the harsh flavor that develops if salt alone is used to cure the meat. It does this by altering water activity and causing dehydration. Once moisture leaves the meat, it is less likely to harbor bacterial growth and cause the meat to spoil.

Be sure to use only food-grade salt. Salt substitutes are less desirable for use in cure mixtures.

Sugar: The main role of sugar in the cure is to improve the meat flavor. It counteracts the harshness of salt and can accelerate the cure process. It also helps the meat to brown as it cooks and caramelizes with the heat to enhance the flavor.

Nitrate/Nitrite (saltpeter): The most important function of nitrite is to prevent the growth of the bacterium, Clostridium botulinum (botulism) that can cause illness and death. It also helps to stabilize the cured reddish-pink color, contribute to the characteristic cured meat flavor, retard the development of rancidity during storage, and prevent the warmed-over flavor in reheated meat.

During curing, nitrate breaks down into nitrite and further to nitric oxide. The nitric oxide can react with compounds in the lean meat to form nitrosamines (which cause cancer) if cured meats are cooked enough to be charred. Despite cancer-causing risk, the Food and Drug Administration has determined that the consumer is at a greater health risk from botulism if nitrite is not used than from cancer if it is used in the cure.

Nitrite should be packaged separately from other cure ingredients prior to cure application. Nitrate is no longer allowed in the brine cure solutions used in other types of hams. But because it provides the advantage of protecting dry-cured hams from Clostridium botulinum, the United States Department of Agricultures permits and encourages the use of it in dry-cured ham. Just be sure not to use more than is recommended.

Chapter 5

STEP BY STEP HOME CURING

In Butler, Tennessee, Howard Courtner's father always told him that the hams must go down in the salt cure in November, the month when cold weather usually blew in to the Appalachian town. "Daddy always said to do it in November, no matter what," he says emphatically.

"It was winter when we began curing our hams," says Wallace Edwards, in Surry, Virginia. "I can remember as a boy that if a hot spell came, we had to scramble around and try to save the hams."

Weather has everything to do with a successfully cured ham, as old-timers well know. The meat needs frosty, just-above-freezing temperatures to allow the salt to slowly seep into the meat and draw moisture out. It then needs the mild temperatures and rising humidity of spring to allow the salt to equalize throughout the meat. Then, warmer summer days age and dry out the ham to create the characteristic cured flavor.

The entire curing process takes a minimum of 70 days to comply with the federal requirements for a country-cured ham. Here's how the process breaks down:

Cure Application:	32 days
Cure Equalization:	14 days
Smoking:	3 days
Aging:	<u>21 days</u>
TOTAL:	70 days

Curing time for a longer-aged Smithfield or long-cured ham:

Cure Application:	40 days
Cure Equalization:	14 days
Smoking:	3 days
Aging:	<u>123 days</u>
TOTAL:	180 days

Follow these basic steps to curing your own hams.

Step 1: Applying the Cure

Traditionally, late December to early January is the best time to put hams in cure if the hams will be cured in outside temperatures. When the dry salt cure is applied to the meat, the meat temperature should be between 35° and 40°F. To use a traditional cure mix, rub 8 pounds of salt per 100 pounds of meat over the entire surface of each ham, including the shank ends. Be sure to coat the exposed lean surfaces that will absorb more of the cure. Make sure a 1/8-inch thick layer covers all surfaces of each ham; then stack hams skin side down to cure.

If you want to use sugar in the cure for a less salty taste, mix 8 pounds of salt and 2 pounds of sugar together to rub into 100 pounds of meat. To add brown sugar to the cure, use 8 pounds of salt, 2 pounds of sugar, and 1 pound of brown sugar per 100 pounds of meat.

Next, apply 2 ounces of sodium nitrate to the exposed lean surfaces of each ham. (You can purchase this at drug stores or it may be included with the commercial cure mix that you can purchase at feed stores.)

Then follow one of two rules of thumb to determine the amount of time to leave the hams in salt cure. Allow the ham to absorb the salt cure a total of 2 days for each pound of ham, or seven days per inch of thickness through the thickest portion of the ham.

Hams cured from January 1 through 15 may be fine cured outdoors in a smokehouse if the temperatures don't vary. Otherwise, you can cure the hams in an old refrigerator or walk-in cooler.

Step 2: Overhauling (optional)

Overhauling simply means to reapply salt to the hams 5 to 7 days after applying the first cure mixture. Reapplying salt is an optional step. To overhaul the hams, use 6 pounds of salt per 100 pounds of meat.

Step 3: Cure Equalization

Wash all cure application ingredients from the hams under running water. This will help dissolve any particles left on the hams and make the ham more receptive to smoke, if you plan to smoke the hams.

Allow the hams to equalize in a temperature of 50° to 55°F and 60% relative humidity. If you put the hams in cure in early January for 30 to 40 days, then spring months are often within this temperature and humidity range.

During the equalization period, the salt slowly penetrates the meat to the bone, which is important for preventing spoilage. It also helps to reduce the saltiness on the outside of the hams.

If possible, the hams should be exposed to slightly higher temperatures at the end of the equalization period to prepare them for the aging cycle.

Step 4: Smoking (optional)

Smoke enhances color and flavor, although it is an optional procedure. Hams to be smoked should be exposed to a temperature of 88° to 92°F for an extended period of time. A traditional smoking period is 24 hours of continuous smoke or 8 hours of smoke for each of 3 to 5 days.

Hang the hams so that they do not touch each other or any other surface. The fire in the smokehouse should be a "cool" smoldering type that produces a large amount of smoke and raises the temperature to

90°F. Continue to smoke the hams until they turn a reddish chestnut color.

Hickory and maple are the most popular woods for smoking, but you can use any hardwood tree (one that sheds leaves in the fall) or any fruit tree such as apple, cherry, plum, or peach. Do not use wood from needle-leaf trees such as pine, cedar, or spruce; these trees emit a resin that causes as bitter odor and taste.

Step 5: Packaging

Once the hams are smoked, you may want to coat them in a layer of ground black pepper. The pepper serves as a natural deterrent to insects. Then wrap the hams in heavy brown grocery bags with no rips or tears. Place the ham in the bag first, then fold down the top of the bag. Tie the top of the bag, then place the ham in another heavy grocery bag, folding and tying the top of the bag. Hang the hams in a clean, dry, well-ventilated room for aging.

Step 6: Aging

This is the most important stage of flavor development for cured hams. Hams should be aged for at least 14 days and up to 1 year, depending on the desired flavor intensity. A controlled environment of 85 to 90°F with 60% relative humidity will speed the flavor development process.

If the hams are aging in a season of fluctuating temperatures, it will take longer to develop the aged flavor. Just remember, the longer the hams age, the dryer the ham, and the stronger and more intense the flavor.

Home-Curing Problems

For a guide to Troubleshooting: Home Curing Problems to Avoid, see Appendix A on Page 151.

Chapter 6

HOME CURING FOR FUN AND PROFIT

Why Would You Home-Cure Hams?

Tiny Guier can walk down the road and buy a country ham from one of Kentucky's best producers. Yet, year after year, he cures about 120 hams in the bright red smokehouse behind his house. "I just like to do it, I guess," he muses about why he continues with the hard work.

Willard Scott, America's best-loved jet-setting weatherman finds himself putting a ham or two in salt almost every fall on his Delaplane, Virginia farm.

"Why do I do it?" asks Scott. "Because of my grandfather. It's the continuity of our culture, the romance of a Southern tradition that everyone relates to that keeps me doing it. In fact, I'll bet some of the ashes in my smokehouse are some of the same ones left by my grandfather when he started curing hams in 1914. I love the idea of that.

"Besides, I don't think there's anything that tastes as good or smells more like home. I can remember how it smelled when I came in the house after my grandmother cooked a country ham; smelling it now reminds me of those days."

And so home-curing continues for the nostalgia, for the preservation of an art, and for the flavor that can't be duplicated. Usually it is the people with rural farm roots and those who have the patience of Job that accept the challenge to home-cure, despite the hard work and risks of losing hams to the whims of nature.

Hog-Killing Day: An Age-Old Tradition

In Cadiz, Kentucky, farmer Tiny Guier carries on another tradition as old as that of country ham. While many farmers have opted to cure the "easy" way by purchasing their fresh hams from a meat house, Tiny enjoys the fellowship of his nearby farmer neighbors at his annual hog-killing day.

"Me and my neighbors, we've been working together long enough that everybody knows their job," says Tiny. "Now we can kill 10 hogs and have everything done up by 1 or 1:30--sausage ground, everything. I go help kill two hogs, and dress them. Then when they hang one up, I stay right there. I make the pork chops or backbone, whatever there is to do then. And then when they get to blocking the hog, I help to trim all the hams," describes Tiny.

The ham trimming job belongs only to Tiny. "They won't let any of them trim a ham but me," he says, shaking his head. His neatly trimmed hams have won many awards in cured ham contests, but he claims no secret for trimming the hams. "I just do it like Dad taught me to," he says, "that's all I can tell you."

So for Tiny and his neighbors, satisfaction and enjoyment comes from working together and a job well done. Though not every ham curer can claim to take their hams from the pen to the table, a few like Tiny, keep the tradition alive and well.

Curing to Sell

If you cure hams in your backyard or on your farm and decide to sell a few, like Tiny, there's another factor to consider that's as tough to deal with as uncertain weather. Home curers must strictly adhere to state and federal laws governing inspection of home-cured meat sold to the public.

If you cure hams just for your own use, then you're free to follow the traditions and methods of your choice. But should you decide to sell hams to others, you will need to follow guidelines required by the United States Department of Agriculture (USDA) and submit to inspections by USDA's Food Safety Inspection Service.

U.S. Congress passed the Wholesome Meat Act and the Wholesome Poultry Act to assure that all beef, pork, lamb, veal, and poultry sold in the United States adheres to a uniform standard of wholesomeness. This law requires a federal or state meat inspection in all operations that sell products.

Although the government requirements are in place to protect the public and ensure safe food, the regulations can be difficult to follow.

In Dahlonega, Georgia, The Smith House Restaurant was once known for serving hams cured on-site. "I cured for years and my father did, too," says owner Freddy Welch. "Country ham was a big thing for us---one of our main meats. But it got hard to deal with the laws for curing our own, so I don't cure anymore and now we serve a different kind of ham in the restaurant."

In Kentucky, Tiny Guier has home-cured hams as a hobby for years. His reputation grew, and people began stopping by his farmhouse to purchase a ham, or asking him to mail one to them. "It's now against the law to ship them across the state lines without federal inspection," says Tiny. "If they want a ham from me, they have to come get it. And the inspector comes by from time to time to make sure I'm not doing anything I'm not supposed to."

Howard Courtner of Butler, Tennessee, ran a family ham-curing business handed down from his father for years. His business's claim to fame was an unsmoked, air-cured country ham. No temperature controls were used throughout any part of the curing process. USDA and state inspectors required him to have concrete floors and a certain type of wood for shelves in the building where the hams were cured and aged. The USDA inspector was required to be on-site when fresh hams were delivered from Iowa and hams were put down in salt. All of Courtner's crew was expected to wear white coats when the hams were put in salt. An inspector visited once a week, sometimes more often. Courtner also kept a carefully mapped chart of the daily recorded temperatures in the building for the inspectors to review.

Selling Within State Boundaries

Most states have developed their own programs for inspecting meat produced within the state lines. Meat inspection programs are paid for by the state and/or federal government instead of the individual companies, so that the inspectors serve as a disinterested party during the inspection process.

If you decide to sell your hams, you'll need to obtain a grant of inspection. To find out laws governing your particular state, or to apply for a grant of inspection, contact your state agricultural department for more information.

Alabama Department of Agriculture
Meat and Poultry Section
1445 Federal Drive
P.O. Box 3336
Montgomery, AL 36109-0336
334-240-7210

Georgia Department of Agriculture
Meat Inspection Section
Room 108, Ag Building
19 Martin Luther King, Jr. Drive
Atlanta, GA 30334
404-656-3673
800-282-5852-Ag Consumer Line/ask for Meat Inspection Division

North Carolina Department of Agriculture
Meat and Poultry Inspection Service
1001 Mail Service Center
Raleigh, NC 27699-1001
919-733-4136

Virginia Department of Agriculture
Meat and Poultry Inspection Division
Washington Building
1100 Bank Street
Richmond, VA 23219
804-786-4569

Kentucky:
Jaime Mercado
USDA District Office
6020 Six Fork Road
Raleigh, NC 27609
919-844-8400

Missouri:
Dr. William Walker
USDA District Office
4920 West 15th Street
Lawrence, KS 66049
785-841-5600

Tennessee:
Mr. Perry Davis
USDA District Office
715 South Pear Orchard Road
Suite 101
Ridgeland, MS 39157
601-965-4312 or 800-647-2484

Where to Get Food Safety Inspection Information

For more information on the USDA meat inspection program, regulations for ham house operations, and for the contact names and phone numbers at USDA district offices: *USDA Meat and Poultry Hotline, Washington, D.C.; **800-535-4555**

*USDA Food Safety Inspection Service web site
www.FSIS.USDA.gov

Marriott and Ockerman

III

Tips For Country Ham Cooks

"I don't think there's anything that tastes as good or smells more like home. I can remember how it smelled when I came in the house after my grandmother cooked a country ham; smelling it now reminds me of those days."

-----Willard Scott,
Delaplane, Virginia

Chapter 7

HOW MAMA COOKED HER HAM:
How to Cut It, Serve It, and Store It

Whole Hams: The Old-Fashioned Way

Just 50 years ago, all you needed to cook a country ham was a cast iron skillet and a cup of coffee, or an old lard stand, a few quilts, and some firewood. The skillet was the ticket to a sizzling slice of ham simmered in coffee to create traditional redeye gravy.

To cook a whole ham, the meat was simmered in water in a large ham cooker, lard stand, or lard can over an outdoor fire or on a wood-burning stove. Once the water came to a boil, the ham container was removed from the heat and covered in old quilts or newspapers, then allowed to continue cooking slowly as the water cooled. It made for a succulent and tender ham ready for shaving into tissue thin slices destined to be piled between tender biscuit halves.

Sometimes the simmered ham would be crusted with sugar and spices or topped with a sweet glaze and then baked, for a special occasion. These glazes became family traditions and specialties that graced many a holiday or special occasion meal.

Home-cured hams varied in salt content, often much higher than the salt content of today's commercially cured hams. But society had yet to become salt-conscious, and cooks rarely bothered to soak the hams to remove excess salt before cooking them.

"Most oldtimers never soaked their hams much," recalls Smith Broadbent III, a third generation retired country ham producer in Cadiz, Kentucky. "I don't remember my grandmother ever soaking hers."

The Lard Can Legacy

Vintage recipes call for a ham boiler or a large lard can for cooking whole country hams. These extra large containers accommodated the especially hefty hams from those early days.

"They used lard cans because everybody had those," says Smith Broadbent. "Back then hogs had a lot of fat; they used it in cooking and people rendered a lot of lard. So everybody had a lard can."

Today, a large, deep kettle with a rack is what most folks use for simmering whole country hams. Some ham experts prefer large stainless steel cookers.

If you'd like to buy a lard stand or lard can for old times' sake, a few places still sell them. Check with your local hardware store; most can locate one to order if they don't have them in stock. Here is a source where lard cans are available: **Brown's Braemar Store,** 613 Highway 321, Hampton, TN 37658; 423-725-2411

A Country Fried Favorite

Years ago, children were sent to the smokehouse on chilly winter mornings to yank a ham from the rafters and saw some slices from the center for the morning's breakfast. The remaining cut halves were then slathered with lard, stuck together and placed back in the flour sack to hang until time to cut more slices for frying.

The thick, salty slices were a regular morning treat with eggs, biscuits, and redeye gravy. Soaking the slices was an option to reduce the salty taste, but most folks liked it just the way it was.

Freddy Welch is a onetime ham curer and second generation owner of the famous Smith House in Dahlonega, Georgia, once known for curing and serving fried country ham on the family style menu. He says most of the slices they served were soaked before cooking to reduce the saltiness.

"I have especially liked learning how the country cooks we've hired over the years cook their hams," says Freddy. "Some soaked the slices in plain warm water before frying them," he explains. "One lady thought it was best to soak the slices in sweet milk for about 30 minutes, but I could never tell the difference in milk and water."

Of course, the most traditional of fried ham was served with redeye gravy. This watery broth was made simply by adding water to the skillet after the ham was fried, and cooking to stir loose the browned bits of ham stuck to the pan. The resulting broth was reddish in color. Adding coffee (usually strong-flavored) is an optional, but time-honored tradition.

Beaten Biscuits: A Southern Tradition

Soft, fluffy biscuits practically define country Southern cooking today. But once upon a time, small porcelain smooth, rock hard biscuits known as "beaten" biscuits were a must have for serving with country ham.

In days when leavening wasn't always available, resourceful Southerners came up with the recipe for a biscuit that required only flour, lard or butter, salt, and cold water. The dough was mixed, then literally beaten to add air (a form of leavening) to the mixture. The result was a hard biscuit that was flaky and tender inside.

Beating the biscuit dough was the key to good beaten biscuits. Cooks designated a smooth-topped tree stump for the process. In pre-Civil War days, a trusted slave was given the job of beating the dough on the stump with a special wooden mallet.

The rule was "beat the dough 300 times for family, 500 times for company." The extra beating ensured extra-flaky layers for the insides of the biscuits.

Years later a machine called a biscuit brake was invented which operated like a wringer washing machine. Instead of being beaten, the dough was passed through rollers many times.

The dough was cut into small rounds, about 1-1/2 inches in diameter. Just before baking, the top of the dough rounds were pricked with fork tines in 2 or 3 rows, giving the baked biscuit its traditional appearance. Beaten biscuits can be made today using a heavy-duty food processor. But Broadbent B & B Foods in

Cadiz, Kentucky, sells them ready-made. You just heat them to serve. To order, call 800-841-2202.

How to Fry It Right

While cooked country ham is best sliced paper thin, slices for frying should be cut about 1/8- to 3/8-inch thick. If you broil, rather than fry it, then slice the ham about 1/2-inch thick. To remove some of the salty taste, you can soak uncooked ham slices in water for about 30 minutes before cooking.

How to Cut It

Unlike other hams, cooked country ham is best when slices are shaved as thin as possible. "My dad had a reputation that he could slice it so thin you could read a newspaper through it," says S. Wallace Edwards, II, a Virginia ham producer. "We stress slicing it thin because thick slices of a 6- to 12-month aged ham are just overpowering."

To get the most attractive slices, Edwards suggests cutting a V-shaped chunk of ham a few inches from the shank (narrow) end of the ham. Then slice the ham, starting at the top and cutting toward the bone at a 45-degree angle.

If the task is just too daunting, you can take your cooked ham to the supermarket butcher or deli; most will slice it for you for a small fee.

Planning for a Party

A country-cured ham provides more servings than other types of ham because the flavor is so intense you don't eat as much of it. Often, it is not the only meat served with the meal. More bland meats such as chicken or seafood, compliment the strong flavor of the ham. Use the chart below to determine what size ham to buy to get the number of servings you need.

Figuring Country Ham Servings

Ham Weight	# Slices	# Servings	# Ham Biscuits
10 pounds	64	25	250
12 pounds	84	33	325

Storing Country Ham

Uncooked country hams can be stored unrefrigerated in a cloth or brown paper sack in a cool, dry place. Never wrap a cooked or uncooked country ham in plastic wrap. After the ham is cut, wrap the remaining portion in brown paper or heavy-duty aluminum foil and store it in the refrigerator.

If you don't plan to cook the ham for a while, then package it in serving portions in heavy-duty aluminum foil or freezer paper and freeze up to three months in the freezer. After three months, the ham is still safe to eat, but the flavor and quality won't be as good.

Cooked country ham should be wrapped in brown paper or aluminum foil and refrigerated. Never use plastic wrap to store ham; it promotes spoilage. Cooked country ham will keep in the refrigerator for up to six weeks.

What To Do With Leftovers

The best thing about a country ham is that you can use every bit of it--all the way to the bone. The nicest slices from the center are used for special meals and frying to serve with red-eye gravy. The smaller slices and crumbles of meat left from a much-carved ham are great for adding to soups, casseroles, serving between biscuits, and even for making appetizers.

Once you've picked all the meat you can from the bone, freeze the leftover ham and use it in one of the recipes in Chapter 10.

Vonnie Edwards, wife of second-generation ham producer S. Wallace Edwards in Surry, Virginia, suggests freezing the broth made from the ham bone. Freeze the broth in ice cube trays, then store the cubes in the freezer. When cooking vegetables or soups, add a few of the frozen cubes for flavor.

Edwards suggests using chopped or ground country ham by stirring it into omelets, scrambled eggs, quiche, pancakes, rice, potato salad, macaroni & cheese, cheese balls, and tossed salad.

Use small, thin strips of leftover ham for a party tray. Wrap 1-inch-wide slices around cheese cubes, melon balls, pineapple chunks, watermelon pickles, or homemade sweet pickle chunks.

In Smithfield, Virginia, Jeanne Groves finds that the tiny pieces are delicious sprinkled on top of home-made pizza.

CHAPTER 8

WHERE TO GET A COUNTRY HAM

What kind of ham do you want? The best country ham comes from where you come from, says Merle Ellis, best known as "The Butcher," a country ham lover and nationally known celebrity.

So which ham should you buy if you've never even tried it? The biggest flavor variable comes with the amount of time the ham is aged; the longer aged hams are stronger flavored.

Other variations in country-cured hams come with the cure mix, which sometimes contains brown or white sugar. Spices in the cure rarely alter the flavor of the meat, but may add to the aroma of the ham.

Smoking also adds some flavor, but the decision to smoke hams follows a definite geographic line. "In west Kentucky and west Tennessee, you couldn't sell a ham that's not smoked," says Kentucky country ham producer Smith Broadbent, III. "People there like the pecan color you get from smoking." S. Wallace Edwards of eastern Virginia, smokes his hams, too. But, in mountainous east Kentucky and east Tennessee, most hams aren't smoked.

If you've never eaten a country ham, you probably want to sink your teeth into a shorter aged ham for starters. A ham cured with some sugar mixed into the salt cure also may counteract the salty taste that can be a shocker for first-time tasters.

But if you're an old-timer who wants to relish a strong taste of tradition, then order a longer-aged (a year or longer) ham. Nancy Newsom of Col. Newsom's Aged Hams says there are two ways to tell if a ham is truly aged. "Look for a dark red rosy color, and white flecks throughout the red meat where the salt crystals have collected during aging," she says.

If you don't have a container large enough to cook a whole ham or don't want to go to the trouble to saw the slices, most producers now sell a variety of convenient country ham products which make it easy to savor the taste without the trouble of cooking it. You can buy whole cooked hams, cooked boneless hams, and uncooked or cooked slices by the pound in supermarkets or by mail.

The most common convenience package is a vacuum-packed bag of slices ready for frying. If the salt content is high enough, these ham slices may be displayed in the stores unrefrigerated. Delis often sell boneless slices of country ham loaves. Some stores sell whole uncooked aged hams, and will cook them upon request.

Contact the retailers listed at the end of this chapter for more information on available convenience products. Some retailers offer a web site or a catalog for more detailed information about their products.

How To Tell If It's A Good Ham

If you order a ham by mail, use the following checklist to determine whether you've received a quality dry-cured ham:

√ Thin, uniform covering of fat
√ Uniform color over outside of ham (maghogany exterior if smoked, very light mahogany if not smoked)
√ Inside meat is uniform red color, possibly with slight pinkish tinge indicating that the meat cured evenly throughout
√ Mold is to be expected, especially on older aged hams

Yikes! There's Mold On My Ham!

Whatever you do, don't throw out the ham if it comes with a coat of mold. To those unaware, mold often forms on the surface of country hams, much as it does on certain aged cheeses. On Smithfield and other older aged hams in particular, you can expect some mold. Just scrub off the mold with warm water and a stiff vegetable brush just before cooking the ham. If it's heavily coated with mold and you don't plan to cook it for a while, scrub the ham with a mixture of vinegar and water, then hang it in a cool, dry place until you're ready to cook it.

MAIL-ORDER HAM SOURCES

GEORGIA

Callaway Gardens
P.O. Box 2000 (Attention: Mail Order Department)
Pine Mountain, GA 31822
800-280-7524 or 706-663-5100
Products: whole uncooked sugar-cured country hams
(not smoked); dry-cured bacon

The Dillard House
768 Franklin Street, P.O. Box 10
Dillard, GA 30537
800-541-0671 or 706-746-5348
Products: country ham

Lord's Sausage & Country Ham
P.O. Box 1000
Dexter, GA 31019
800-342-6002 or 912-875-3101 or
FAX: 478-875-3039
Products: sausage and country ham

KENTUCKY

Broadbent's B & B Food Products, Inc.
6321 Hopkinsville Road
Cadiz, KY 42211
800-841-2202
FAX: 270-235-9601

Products: sugar-cured, hickory-smoked country ham, bacon, sausage; long-cure hams available; beaten biscuits, other ham products. Catalog available.
http://www.Broadbenthams.com

Col. Newsom's Aged Hams
127 North Highland Avenue
Princeton, KY 42445
270-365-2482
http://www.newsomscountryham.com
Products: whole, uncooked hams aged 1+years, cured with salt & brown sugar, hickory smoked

Father's Country Hams
P.O. Box 99
Bremen, KY 42325
270-525-3554
FAX: 270-525-3333
Products: aged country hams, cured bacon, cooked hams, smoked sausage

Finchville Farms
P.O. Box 56
5157 Taylorsville Road
Finchville, KY 40022
800-678-1521 or 502-834-7952
FAX: 502-834-7095
Products: sugar-cured, fully-aged country hams; fully-cooked boneless country hams, country bacon, packaged country ham slices and seasoning meats

Harper's Country Hams
P.O. Box 122
2955 US Hwy 51 North
Clinton, KY 42031
800-264-3380 or 270-653-2081
FAX: 270-653-2409
http://www.hamtastic.com
Products: country ham, country bacon, barbecue pork ribs and turkey, smoked country sausage, country ham jerky

Meacham Hams
705 O'Nan Dyer Road
Sturgis, KY 42459-9735
800-552-3190 or 502-333-6924
FAX: 502-333-4131
http://www.meachamhams.com
Products: country ham

Scott Hams
1301 Scott Road
Greenville, KY 42345
270-338-3402
FAX: 502-338-6643
Products: country ham, fully-cooked or uncooked; country bacon, and smoked sausage

MISSOURI

Burger's Smokehouse
32819 Highway 87 South
California, MO 65018

800-203-4424 or 573-796-3134
FAX: 573-796-3137
http://www.smokehouse.com
Products: cured, smoked hams, poultry, and other meats

NORTH CAROLINA

Goodnight Brothers
P.O. Box 287
172 Industrial Park Dr.
Boone, NC 28607
800-828-4934 or 828-264-8892 or
FAX: 828-264-0650
http://www.goodnightbrothers.com
Products: country ham

Hobes Country Hams
P.O. Box 350
389 Elledgemill Road
North Wilkesboro, NC 28659
336-670-3401
FAX: 336-670-3631
Products: country ham

Johnston County Country Hams
204 North Brightleaf Boulevard
P. O. Box 489
Smithfield, NC 27577
800-543-4267 or 919-934-8054
FAX: 919-934-1091
http://www.countrycuredhams.com

Products: sugar-cured, smoked uncooked country hams; cooked spiral-sliced country hams

Ralph Medlin & Sons Inc.
P.O. Box 655
700 Lincoln Street
Benson, NC 27504
919-894-2626
Products: country ham

Mom 'n' Pop's Smokehouse
P.O. Box 820
Claremont, NC 28610
828-459-3126
877-667-4426
FAX: 828-459-3138
http://www.momnpops.net
Products: country ham and bacon

Thomas Brothers Country Hams
1852 Gold Hill Road
Asheboro, NC 27203
336-672-0337
FAX: 336-672-1782
Products: country ham; retail and food service items

Wayco Hams
P.O. Box 841
Goldsboro, NC 27533
800-962-2614 or 919-735-3962
FAX: 919-734-4080
http://www.waycohams.com

Products: country ham, smoked turkey, honey baked hams, country side meat

PENNSYLVANIA

Rotz Meats Country Butcher Shop
CR 75 Box 30
McConnellsburg, PA 17233
717-485-3467
FAX: 717-485-0265
http://www.rotzmeats.com
Products: pork, beef, and country-cured ham and bacon

TENNESSEE

Clifty Farms/Tennessee Valley Ham Company
P.O. Box 1146
Paris, TN 38242
800-748-9373 or 901-642-9740
FAX: 901-642-7129
http://www.cliftyfarm.com
Products: country ham--whole line, cooked boneless ham, barbecue, jerky

Cracker Barrel by Mail
305 Hartmann Dr.
Lebanon, TN 37088
800-333-9566

Products: whole country ham, uncooked or cooked and spiral-sliced, cooked and spiral-sliced country ham halves, sampler and gift sets including country ham steaks

G &W Hamery Country Hams
411 West Lytle Street
Murfreesboro, TN 37130
615-893-9712
Products: country ham, aged country hams

MarTenn Country Hams
P.O. Box 288
Martin, TN 38237
902-587-3803
FAX: 901-587-9809
Products: country ham

Miller's Country Hams
7110 Highway 190
Dresden, TN 38225
800-622-0606 or 901-364-3940
FAX: 901-364-5338
Products: sliced and whole country ham

Tripp Country Hams
P.O. Box 527
Brownville, TN 38012
800-471-9814 or 731-772-2130
FAX: 731-772-6798
http://www.countryhams.com
Products: country ham and country bacon

VIRGINIA

S. Wallace Edwards & Sons, Inc.
P.O. Box 25
11455 Rolfe Highway.
Surry, VA 23883
800-222-4267 or 757-294-3121
FAX: 757-294-5378
http://www.virginiatraditions.com
Products: hickory-smoked, pepper-coated country ham, bacon & sausage

Basse's Choice Catalogue
P.O. Box 250
Portsmouth, VA 23705
800-292-2773
Fax: 757-673-7003
http://www.smithfieldhams.com
Products: salt-cured country ham and pepper-coated genuine Smithfield ham smoked with hickory, apple, and oak woods, uncooked and fully cooked; bacon, picnics, pork, chicken and beef barbecue

The Smithfield Catalog
P.O. Box 250
Portsmouth, VA 23705
800-926-8448
Fax: 757-673-7004
http://www.smithfieldhams.com
Products: salt-cured country ham and pepper-coated genuine Smithfield ham smoked with hickory, apple, and oak woods, uncooked and fully cooked; bacon, picnics, pork, chicken and beef barbecue

The Smithfield Collection
P.O. Box 250
Portsmouth, VA 23705
800-628-2242
Fax: 757-673-7005
http://www.smithfieldcollection.com
Products: salt-cured country ham and pepper-coated genuine Smithfield ham smoked with hickory, apple, and oak woods, uncooked and fully cooked; bacon, picnics, pork, chicken and beef barbecue

R. M. Felts Packing Co.
P. O. Box 199
Ivor, VA 23866
757-859-6131
Fax: 757-859-6381
Products: salt-cured and smoked country ham

Chapter 9

UNFORGETTABLE
COUNTRY HAM MENUS

Look to the experts---producers and restauran-
teurs who have made country ham a traditional part of
their meals for generations---to plan some delicious
ways to serve this delicacy. Here are some that feature
or complement country ham and their favorite ways to
put country ham on the table. Some menu items include recipes, found in Chapter 10, on page number
noted in parentheses.

QUICK & EASY ITALIAN APPETIZER BUFFET
Sarah Brown, Johnston County Hams
Smithfield, North Carolina

Sarah Brown, wife of second generation ham
producer Rufus Brown, says that country ham is on her
menu any time she needs a quick and easy meal for
guests. "I serve an Italian appetizer buffet that requires
practically no cooking," says Sarah. "It's not your typical Southern meal, but when I entertain, I want to enjoy
my guests, not spend time in the kitchen."

To make the menu easier on the cook, Sarah cuts
up serving-size pieces of packaged pre-sliced cooked
country ham (she uses three or four 8-ounce packages
to serve 6), buys pickled asparagus and marinated olives from a local deli, and slices a lemon pound cake
purchased from the bakery.

Thin-Sliced Cooked Country Ham
Chick Peas in Olive Oil (Page 129)
Chilled Pickled Asparagus
Marinated Olives
Tomato Slices with Melted Mozzarella (Page 130)
Chutney Cheese Round (Page 130)
Assorted Crackers
Bruschetta (Page 141)
Wine; Water
Lemon Pound Cake
Fresh Berries in Season
Coffee
MENU SERVES 6

NORTH GEORGIA BREAKFAST SMORGASBORD
John Dillard, The Dillard House
Dillard, Georgia

For almost a century, the Dillard family has been curing hams and serving a Georgia mountain-style breakfast at their family inn and restaurant. This menu is a collection of the offerings at the all-you-can-eat family style meal served at the restaurant. The recipes are from *The Dillard House Cookbook and Mountain Guide*, a compilation of generations of Dillard family recipes. As is Southern custom, the menu offers a variety of breads and meats from which to choose. To prepare a traditional country ham breakfast at home, don't worry about serving the whole menu; just pick your favorites and enjoy!

Honeydew Melon Slices
Scrambled Eggs
Cheese Grits (Page 131)
Fried Apple Rings (Page 131)
Country Ham with Red Eye Gravy (Page 126)
Link Sausage (Page 127)
Pork Tenderloin (Page 127)
Buttermilk Biscuits with Sausage Gravy (Page 142)
Silver Dollar Pancakes (Page 144)
Butter, Sourwood Honey or Syrup
Blueberry Muffins (Page 145)
Cinnamon Rolls (Page 146)
Orange Juice , Coffee
MENU SERVES 8 TO 10

VIRGINIA FAMILY DINNER
Vonnie Edwards, S. Wallace Edwards & Sons, Inc.
Surry, Virginia

"This menu is so ordinary," explains Vonnie Edwards, wife of ham producer Wallace Edwards. "But it's one our family seems to enjoy." Apples are a must with country ham, particularly in Virginia where the two are paired as readily as eggs and ham or peanut butter and jelly. Vonnie says her Sweet Potato Casserole is a regular hit at church socials and the applesauce cake is an old family favorite, handed down from Wallace's grandmother, Olive Connor Jester.

Fruit Shrub (Page 132)
Fried Ham Slices with Red Eye "Sloppy" Gravy (Page 125)
Corn Pudding (Page 132)
Sweet Potato Casserole (Page 133)
Green Beans and Bacon (Page 134)
Fried Apples (Page 134)
Sunshine Salad (Page 135)
Homemade Rolls (Page 141)
Grandmother Jester's Applesauce Cake (Page 149)
Iced Tea
Menu serves 4

TENNESSEE CHRISTMAS CELEBRATION
Lynne Tolley, Miss Mary Bobo's Boarding House
Lynchburg, Tennessee

This menu is straight from Lynne Tolley, grand-niece of Jack Daniels and proprietor of Miss Mary Bobo's Boarding House. "We cook with Jack Daniel's Whiskey in as many ways as possible here," says Lynne. If you can't get to Miss Mary Bobo's for the Christmas menu served there each December, you can use the recipes below to create your own celebration at home.

Baked Country Ham, Jack Daniels Glaze (Pages 107; 110)
Baked Turkey with Cornbread Dressing (Page 136)
Intoxicated Cranberry Relish (Page 137)
Macaroni and Cheese (Page 138)
Tipsy Sweet Potatoes (Page 139)
Fried Okra (Page 139)
Hot Rolls   Butter
Iced Tea   Water
Jack Daniel's Brownies and Glaze (Page 148)
Coffee
MENU SERVES 6 TO 8

IV

Ham and All the Trimmings:

Favorite Recipes for Today's Cooks

Chapter 10

HAM AND ALL THE TRIMMINGS: FAVORITE RECIPES FOR TODAY'S COOKS

Some of these recipes come from the menus in Chapter 9, plus many additional delicious recipes have been added.

HAM, HAM AND MORE HAM

HOW TO COOK A WHOLE HAM

Old-Fashioned Simmered Whole Country Ham

The National Country Ham Association has simplified the once arduous task of cooking a country ham. Remember the 5 "S's" in this recipe to cook a country ham that is tender, juicy, and not too salty: Saw, Soak, Simmer, Slice and Serve. Simmering the ham is a favorite cooking method with cooks in all country ham-producing regions and the most similar to the lard stand method used years ago.

1 (12- to 14-pound) whole uncooked country ham
Whole cloves
2 cups firmly packed brown sugar
Pineapple slices (optional)

Saw off about 5 inches of the hock or narrow end (also called the shank) from ham. If you're not equipped to do this at home, your local supermarket butcher may do it for you. They'll often do it free of charge or for a small fee. (Be sure to save the hock to simmer for making broth for soup or to season country-style vegetables. The hock may be frozen for later use.)

Place ham in a stainless steel or enamel kettle or pot large enough to allow ham to be covered by at least 2 or 3 inches of water. Add cold water to above top of the ham; soak 24 hours. If ham is an older aged one (aged 9 months or more), then soak up to 72 hours, changing the water at least 2 or 3 times.

Drain off soaking water; place a rack in the bottom of kettle. Add ham and cover again with water, making sure water is 2 to 3 inches above the top of the ham. Heat the water over high heat just until it begins to simmer (do not boil). Reduce heat and allow water to simmer, uncovered, 15 minutes per pound (about 3 to 3-1/2 hours) or until meat thermometer registers 160°F. Add water as necessary during cooking.

Allow ham to cool in cooking liquid. Remove ham from the kettle and discard cooking liquid.

Use a sharp knife to slit the rind (skin) beginning at the hock end and cutting to the butt end. Peel the skin away from the ham; trim away excess fat. Leave 1/4-inch layer of fat if you plan to score the ham and coat with a dry sugar glaze. To glaze, place the trimmed ham in a large roaster.

To coat the ham with a traditional brown sugar glaze, score the fat layer on the ham surface into 1- to 2-inch squares in a diamond pattern. Press whole cloves into scored fat. Coat ham with a layer of brown sugar. If desired, secure pineapple slices over the ham surface in a decorative design.

Bake, uncovered, at 425°F for 10 to 15 minutes or until lightly browned and crusty. Yield: 30 to 35 servings

Simmered Whole Kentucky Country Ham

This recipe from the Kentucky Extension Service uses brown sugar or molasses to counteract country ham's natural salt flavor.

1 (12- to 14-pound) whole uncooked country ham
Brown sugar or molasses

Remove hock and soak ham as directed in recipe for Old-Fashioned Simmered Country Ham. Drain off soaking water.

Place ham on a rack in a large kettle or pot. Add water to cover ham at least 2 to 3 inches. Add one tablespoon brown sugar or molasses for each 1 quart of water.

Heat water over high heat until it begins to simmer (do not boil); reduce heat and simmer 15 minutes per pound of ham (about 3 to 3-1/2 hours) or until meat thermometer registers 160°F. (Insert thermometer in thickest part of ham, making sure it does not touch fat or bone.) Add water as necessary during cooking.

Allow ham to cool in cooking liquid; remove from kettle and discard liquid. Glaze as desired. (See glaze recipes, page 108.) Yield: 30 to 35 servings

Boneless Florida-Style Whole Country Ham

Mila Freeman Hodge of Sarasota, Florida, shared this favorite recipe with Harper's Country Hams in Clinton, Kentucky. She found a unique way to use her state's native oranges to flavor her country ham.

1 (12- to 14-pound) whole uncooked country ham
Orange juice
Apple cider
1 cup firmly packed brown sugar
2 tablespoons prepared mustard
3 to 4 tablespoons pineapple juice

Remove hock and soak ham as directed in recipe for Old-Fashioned Simmered Country Ham. Drain off soaking liquid.

Place ham on a rack in a large kettle or pot. Add equal amounts of orange juice and apple cider to cover ham by at least 2 to 3 inches.

Heat juices over high heat just until it begins to simmer (do not boil). Reduce heat and allow juices to simmer, uncovered, 15 minutes per pound (about 3 to 3-1/2 hours) or until meat thermometer inserted in ham registers 160°F. (Insert meat thermometer in thickest part of ham, making sure it does not touch fat or bone.) Add juice or cider as necessary during cooking.

Allow ham to cool in cooking liquid. Remove ham from kettle and discard cooking liquid.

Use a sharp knife to slit the rind (skin) beginning at the hock end and cutting to the butt end. Peel the skin away from the ham; trim away excess fat, leaving a 1/4-inch layer of fat to cover ham.

To bone ham, use a very sharp knife to slit ham lengthwise down to the bone, especially working knife around joint portion to loosen. Remove bone. Roll meat jellyroll fashion; tie with strong cotton string.

Combine brown sugar and mustard; add enough pineapple juice to form a thick paste. Coat ham with sugar-mustard paste.

Place coated ham in a roaster. Bake, uncovered, at 425°F for 10 to 15 minutes or until lightly browned and crusty. Yield: 30 to 35 servings

Baked Country Ham with Glaze

Cut off hock, clean whole ham thoroughly with a brush and rough cloth. Trim off any dark, dry edges and discolored fat. Since hams have a dry cure, soaking in water around 8 hours before cooking is often desirable.

Place ham, skin side up, on a rack in an open pan. Start ham covered with roaster lid or aluminum foil in a 375°F oven for 1 hour. Reduce heat to 200°F and cook until the center of the ham registers 160°F on a meat thermometer. This will take about 45 to 50 minutes per pound for whole hams. Hams continue to cook after removal from oven. For well done meat, internal temperature should reach 170°F. Remove skin and allow ham to cool slightly. Serve as is or glaze ham before serving.

To glaze, use a sharp knife to remove skin from cooked ham. Score fat beneath skin in a diamond pattern with a sharp knife. Bake at 350°F for 30 minutes, basting occasionally with glaze, or until browned.

Carving tip: Baked hams are much easier to slice when chilled. Cut slices thin and perpendicular to the bone.

Baked Whole Country Ham

Here's Lynne Tolley's recipe for the baked ham served at Miss Mary BoBo's Boarding House Restaurant in Lynchburg, Tennessee, and from her cookbook, "Jack Daniel's The Spirit of Tennessee Cookbook."

1 (12- to 14-pound) whole uncooked country ham
Ingredients for glaze, optional

Remove hock and soak ham as directed in recipe for Old-Fashioned Simmered Country Ham. Drain off soaking liquid.

Place ham skin side up, on a rack in a large roaster; cover with foil. Bake at 375°F for 1 hour. Reduce heat to 200 to 225°F and bake, uncovered, 45 to 50 minutes per pound (about 9 to 10 hours) or until a meat thermometer registers 160°F. (Insert meat thermometer in thickest part of ham, making sure it does not touch fat or bone.)

Remove from oven and allow ham to cool until a meat thermometer registers 170°F for well-done ham. Remove skin and allow ham to cool slightly. Serve as is or add glaze. Slice thin to serve hot or cold. Yield: 30 to 35 servings

COUNTRY HAM TOPPINGS

Crunchy crusts, shiny glazes, and spice and fruit decorations give whole country hams the stately appearance that it deserves. The coatings add a touch of sweetness to counteract the salty flavor. Try one of these glazes or crusts on any simmered or baked whole ham.

To Glaze Ham:

Using a sharp knife, remove skin and fat, leaving 1/4-inch layer of fat over ham. Score fat.

Combine brown sugar and fruit juice, or combine crushed, drained pineapple and honey, depending on your preference. Spread glaze mixture over ham. Insert whole cloves 1 inch apart over glazed portion of ham.

Bake at 350°F for 30 minutes or until glaze is lightly browned.

Brown Sugar-Bread Crumb Crust:

Combine 1 cup firmly packed brown sugar and 1/4 cup fine dry breadcrumbs. Press over a whole cooked country ham. Broil on lowest rack of oven 4 to 5 minutes or until sugar is caramelized.

Fruity Brown Sugar Crust

Pat 1 to 2 cups firmly packed brown sugar over a whole cooked country ham. Brush fruit juice, sweet cider, or pickled peach juice over sugar-coated ham. Broil on lowest rack of oven 4 to 5 minutes or until sugar is caramelized, basting occasionally with juice.

Pineapple-Brown Sugar Glaze

Drain juice from 1 (8-ounce) can crushed pineapple, reserving juice. Combine pineapple and 1 cup firmly packed brown sugar; spread mixture over a whole cooked country ham. Broil on lowest rack of oven 4 to 5 minutes or until glaze is melted, basting often with reserved pineapple juice.

Sweet-Tart Mustard Glaze

Spread prepared mustard in a thin layer over whole cooked country ham. Sprinkle a generous amount of brown sugar over mustard. Broil on lowest rack of oven 4 to 5 minutes or until sugar is caramelized.

Pineapple Glaze

Blend 1 (8-ounce) can drained, crushed pineapple and 2/3 cup firmly packed brown sugar; pour over fat side of cooked whole country ham. Using wooden toothpicks, secure maraschino cherries and canned pineapple slices over fat side of ham in a decorative pattern. Bake at 400°F until golden brown.

Jack Daniel's Ham Glaze

1 cup orange juice
1/4 cup Jack Daniel's Whiskey
1/2 cup firmly packed brown sugar
1 tablespoon ground ginger
1/2 teaspoon whole cloves

Combine all ingredients in a saucepan over medium-high heat; bring to a boil. Reduce heat to low and simmer 20 minutes or until mixture reaches a syrup-like consistency. Use to glaze baked ham.

Honey Glaze for Baked Ham

Combine 1 cup honey and 1/4 cup maraschino cherry juice. (May add chopped cherries, if desired.) Brush honey mixture over ham as it bakes.

Elegant Fruit Topping for Baked Ham

Using wooden toothpicks, secure any combination of fresh or canned pineapple slices, thin slices of unpeeled oranges, lemons, or limes, and maraschino cherries to fat side of a whole country ham. In a small saucepan, combine 1 cup firmly packed brown sugar and 1/2 cup water; bring to a boil over medium-high heat, stirring constantly. Cook 3 to 5 minutes, stirring constantly, until mixture is thick and syrup-like. Use sugar syrup to baste fruit-topped ham as it bakes.

Tripp's Slow-Fried Country Ham
with Red-Eye Gravy

This recipe from Tripp's Country Hams in Brownsville, Tennessee, is as traditional as it gets.

1 (1/4- to 1/3-inch) thick slice uncooked country ham
1/2 to 3/4 cup water
2 tablespoons strong-brewed coffee (optional)

Place a seasoned cast-iron skillet over low heat. Place ham in skillet; add enough water to cover bottom of skillet. Cook 10 minutes, turning often. Remove ham from skillet; keep warm.

Add coffee and remaining water to skillet. Cook, stirring often, over medium heat 3 to 5 minutes or until gravy is reddish in color. Serve over biscuits and ham. Yield: 1 serving

Cola-Fried Country Ham Slices

1 (1/8-inch-thick) slice uncooked country ham
Cola-flavored or lemon-lime flavored carbonated
beverage
Water

Place a heavy skillet over medium-low heat.
Add ham to skillet; pour just enough cola and water
over ham to cover bottom of skillet. (Do not use too
much cola or it will burn.)

Cook ham 5 to 8 minutes, turning often. Remove from skillet and serve hot. Yield: 1 serving

Westphalia Inn Skillet-Fried Ham

Melody Buersmeyer, owner of the Westphalia Inn Restaurant in Westphalia, Missouri, says this is the way country ham has been fried at the inn for more than 50 years. She says the key to keeping it from tasting salty is to scrape the meat to remove gritty shavings from the bone and marrow and the salt from the rind, which spreads to the meat surface when slices are cut.

2 (3/16-inch-thick) slices uncooked country ham from a
20-pound ham
1/4 to 1/2 cup lard

Using a dull knife, scrape both sides of ham slices to remove marrow and bone grit from meat. Rinse ham.

Cut rind from ham slices, leaving a small amount of fat; remove round bones. Cut slices into serving size pieces.

Place a cast-iron skillet over high heat until hot. Add 1/4 cup lard (enough to cover bottom of skillet with 1/8-inch melted lard). When lard melts, add ham slices to skillet in a single layer, being sure to cover entire surface of skillet with ham slices. (This prevents grease from popping out of skillet.)

Cook 1 to 2 minutes or until ham pieces begin to bubble and lift from skillet. Turn ham and cook an additional 1 to 2 minutes. Remove from skillet. Yield: 2 servings

Broiled Kentucky Country Ham

1 (1/2-inch) thick center-cut slice uncooked country ham

Trim edges of ham, removing skin, if necessary. Place slice on rack of a broiler pan.

Broil 6 inches from heat for 7 minutes; turn ham and broil an additional 6 minutes or until ham is done. Yield: 1 serving

Grilled Country Ham Steaks
with Raisin and Cranberry Sauce

Ham slices become steaks when cut a little thicker. The grilled-outdoors flavor and colorful glaze make this recipe from Miller Country Ham in Dresden, Tennessee, special enough for company.

2 (1-inch-thick) country ham steaks, about 1 pound each
Whole cloves
1/2 cup firmly packed brown sugar
2 tablespoons cornstarch
1-1/2 cups cranberry juice
1/2 cup orange juice
1/2 cup seedless raisins

Score fat on edges of ham steaks at intervals of about 2 inches; insert 2 or 3 cloves into fat on each slice. Set ham aside.

Combine brown sugar and cornstarch in a saucepan; add cranberry juice, stirring until mixture is smooth. Stir in orange juice and raisins. Place saucepan over medium-high heat and cook, stirring constantly, until mixture boils.

Continue boiling for one minute, stirring constantly, or until mixture thickens. Remove from heat, cover, and set aside.

Place ham steaks over low heat on a rack of a gas grill. Place steaks away from hottest part of grill. Cook 15 minutes; turn steaks and brush liberally with cranberry glaze. Cook an additional 10 minutes. Turn steaks again and brush with glaze. Cook an additional 2 minutes or to desired degree of doneness. Place ham on a serving platter; serve with remaining glaze. Yield: 8 servings

Ham & Cheese Muffins

This recipe from Johnston County Hams in Smithfield, North Carolina, is a breakfast meal-in-one.

2 cups all-purpose flour
1 tablespoon baking powder
1/2 teaspoon salt
1 egg
1 cup buttermilk
1/4 cup canola or vegetable oil
8 ounces diced, cooked country ham
1-1/4 cup grated sharp Cheddar cheese

Combine flour, baking powder, and salt in a large mixing bowl. Set aside.

Combine egg, buttermilk, and oil in a small mixing bowl; whisk until blended. Stir in ham and cheese.

Make a well in center of flour mixture; pour egg mixture in center of well. Stir mixture just until combined (do not overmix).

Spoon batter into greased and floured muffin pans. Bake at 400°F for 20 minutes or until golden brown. Yield: 12 muffins

Country Ham Biscuits

2 cups all-purpose flour
1 tablespoon plus 1 teaspoon baking powder
2 tablespoons shortening
3/4 cup milk
1/2 cup ground cooked country ham

Combine flour and baking powder in a large bowl; stir in ham. Cut in shortening with a pastry blender until mixture resembles the texture of coarse cornmeal. Stir in milk, mixing as little as possible.

Turn dough on onto a lightly floured surface. Pat out dough to an even thickness. Cut dough with a 3-inch biscuit cutter and place on a lightly greased baking sheet. Bake at 425°F for 10 minutes or until lightly browned. Yield: 12 to 14 biscuits

Country Ham & Cheese Grits Souffle

2 cups cooked grits
1 tablespoon butter
2 eggs
2 tablespoons milk
1 cup shredded sharp Cheddar cheese
8 ounces diced, cooked country ham

Combine cooked grits and butter. Set aside to cool.

Combine eggs and milk; add to cooled grits. Stir in cheese and ham; pour into a lightly greased 1-quart casserole dish. Bake at 375°F for 45 minutes or until top is light golden brown. Yield: 4 servings

Country Ham Salad

2 cups finely chopped, cooked country ham
1 cup salad dressing or mayonnaise
1 tablespoon sugar
1/2 cup finely chopped celery
1/2 cup sweet pickle relish
1/2 teaspoon paprika
1 teaspoon black pepper

Combine all ingredients in a large bowl. Serve on lettuce leaves or on bread as a sandwich spread. Yield: about 8 servings

Country Ham-Stuffed Apples

Merle Ellis, "The Butcher," shares this country ham side dish favorite from his kitchen. The syndicated columnist and cooking show host has served as the national spokesperson for the National Country Ham Association.

1/3 cup raisins
1 tablespoon Jack Daniel's whiskey
1 cup finely chopped cooked country ham
3 tablespoons butter, softened
1/4 cup chopped pecans
3 tablespoons brown sugar
4 large baking apples, peeled and cored
2 tablespoons lemon juice
1/4 cup cider vinegar

In a medium bowl, soak raisins in whiskey about 30 minutes, stirring often. Add ham, butter, pecans, and brown sugar to raisins and whiskey.

Place apples in a lightly greased baking dish; sprinkle lemon juice in each apple cavity. Divide ham equally among apples and stuff into cavities. Bake at 350°F for 40 to 45 minutes, basting apples occasionally with vinegar. Yield: 4 servings

Ham Waldorf

4 apples, peeled and chopped
1 cup chopped, cooked country ham
1 cup diced celery
1 cup seedless green grapes, halved or raisins
1/2 cup chopped pecans
3/4 cup mayonnaise

Combine all ingredients in a large bowl; chill and serve on lettuce leaves. Yield: 6 servings

Country Ham Spread

2 (8-ounce) packages cream cheese, softened
1 cup sour cream
1/2 to 1 cup chopped cooked country ham
1/4 cup finely minced onion
1/2 teaspoon garlic powder
1 tablespoon butter
1 cup chopped pecans
1/2 teaspoon Worcestershire sauce

Combine all ingredients in a medium bowl. Serve with crackers and/or raw vegetables. Yield: about 1-1/2 cups

Spinach & Country Ham Salad

1 (10-ounce) package fresh spinach leaves, washed and drained
1 red onion, sliced into rings
1/4 pound cooked country ham, cut into thin strips
2 hard-cooked eggs, sliced
1/2 cup vinegar
1 cup vegetable oil
1/4 cup plus 2 tablespoons sugar
1 teaspoon celery seed
Salt
Black pepper
3/4 cup seasoned croutons

Combine spinach, onion rings, and country ham strips in a large bowl, tossing lightly to mix. Set aside.

Combine vinegar and next 6 ingredients in a container or jar with a tight fitting lid.

Shake to mix.

Just before serving, add dressing to spinach mixture, tossing lightly to mix. Top with egg slices and croutons. Yield: 6 servings

Note: If desired, arrange salad in individual salad bowls, and pass the dressing. For additional color and flavor, add cherry tomato slices or strips of Cheddar cheese.

Hot Brown Sandwich

This sandwich is a country ham version of the traditional Kentucky Hot Brown casserole which features turkey.

1/3 cup butter
1 medium onion, chopped (about 3/4 cup)
1/3 cup all-purpose flour
3 cups milk, warmed
1 teaspoon salt
1/2 teaspoon crushed red pepper
2 eggs, beaten
1/4 pound processed American cheese, cubed
1 tablespoon butter
4 strips cooked country ham
4 slices cooked chicken or turkey
Parmesan cheese
Paprika
4 slices bread, toasted

Melt 1/3 cup butter in a skillet over medium-high heat. Add onion, and cook, stirring constantly, until tender. Add flour to skillet, stirring until smooth. Add milk, salt, and red pepper to skillet, stirring well.

Reduce heat to medium and stir in eggs, processed cheese, and remaining 1 tablespoon butter. Cook, stirring constantly, just until mixture comes to a simmer (do not boil). Remove from heat.

Arrange toast on oven-proof individual serving plates; top with chicken. For each serving, spoon one-fourth of sauce over chicken. Top servings evenly with country ham and Parmesan cheese. Sprinkle paprika over sandwiches.

Broil sandwiches 5 inches from heat for 1 minute or just until sauce begins to bubble. Yield: 4 sandwiches

Smithfield Ham Appetizer Spread on Vegetables

Jeanne C. Groves of Smithfield, Virginia is known for her creative use of country ham. These unique appetizers are a good way to use leftover ham and impress your guests.

1/3 cup minced cooked country ham
1/3 cup chopped green onions
1/3 cup grated Parmesan cheese
1/2 cup mayonnaise

Combine all ingredients. Spread on zucchini slices (1/4-inch-thick) or tomato slices (1/2-inch thick) or spoon into mushroom caps.

Place bread or vegetables topped with ham spread on a greased baking sheet. Bake at 350°F for 15 to 20 minutes. Serve immediately. Yield: about 2 dozen appetizers

Note: Spread ham mixture on English muffin halves or French bread slices to serve at brunch.

Country Ham Balls

If you like party sausage balls, you'll love this version using country ham instead of sausage.

1 pound cooked country ham, ground
2 cups (8 ounces) shredded Cheddar cheese
1/2 cup Bisquick baking mix
1/4 cup water

Combine all ingredients, mixing until combined. Form mixture into 1-inch balls; place on an ungreased baking sheets.

Bake ham balls at 350°F for 20 to 25 minutes or until lightly browned. Serve hot. Yield: 3 to 4 dozen

Note: Serve with toothpicks for easy handling. These are best served hot!

Country Ham and Cheese Log

1 (8-ounce) package cream cheese, softened
1 tablespoon mayonnaise
1/2 cup chopped chutney
1 cup ground cooked country ham
1 cup chopped pecans
Maraschino cherries
Crackers

Combine cream cheese and next 3 ingredients, mixing well. Shape mixture into a log.

Sprinkle pecans on waxed paper; roll ham log in pecans. Wrap ham log in foil, and chill until firm. Garnish ham log with cherries and serve with crackers. Yield: 6 to 8 servings

Fried Ham Slices with Red Eye "Sloppy" Gravy

2 (1/4-inch-thick) slices uncooked Virginia ham
1/4 water
1/2 cup water

Wash ham slices and trim off skin. Place ham slices in a large, heavy skillet, and add 1/4 cup water. Cook on both sides over medium heat until water evaporates and ham is lightly browned. (To prevent tough meat, do not overcook.) Transfer ham to a serving platter.

Add 1/2 cup water (or 1/4 cup water and 1/4 cup black coffee) to skillet drippings; bring to a boil. Serve with ham. Yield: 4 servings

Country Ham Gravy

1/2 cup country ham tidbits or ground cooked country ham
1 tablespoon vegetable shortening or vegetable oil
1/4 cup all-purpose flour
2-1/2 cups milk
Salt and pepper to taste

Melt shortening or heat oil in a heavy skillet over medium heat; add ham and cook 2 to 3 minutes, stirring occasionally.

Add flour to skillet, and cook, stirring constantly, to form a paste. Gradually add milk, stirring constantly. (Add less milk for a thicker gravy, more for a thinner gravy.) Add salt and pepper to taste. Serve hot over ham and biscuits. Yield: about 2 cups

Fat-Free Ham Broth

1 meaty country ham bone
Water

Place ham bone in a large kettle. Add water to cover bone by at least 2 inches. Bring to a boil over high heat; reduce heat and simmer 1 to 2 hours.

Remove ham from broth and discard. Allow broth to cool, then cover and chill. Strain broth and discard fat and meat bits that remain in strainer. Broth can be frozen in quart containers and used later. Use broth to season vegetables, beans, and as soup base.

Country Ham with Red Eye Gravy

1 cup bacon drippings
4 large slices country ham
1 tablespoon brown sugar
1/2 cup black coffee
1/2 cup water

Place a large, heavy skillet over medium-low heat, and add bacon drippings. Cook ham slices in drippings just until browned, turning to brown both sides; remove ham from skillet.

Add sugar, coffee, and water to skillet; bring to a boil. Serve on grits, biscuits, or scrambled eggs.
Yield: 6 to 8 servings

Note: Red Eye Gravy may be stored, covered, in the refrigerator and reheated to serve.

OTHER PORK DISHES

Link Sausage

Add desired number of fresh sausage links and 1/2 cup water to a baking dish. Bake at 325°F for 12 to 15 minutes, or until sausage is browned. Drain; serve hot.

Pork Tenderloin

6 (1/2-inch-thick) slices pork tenderloin
1-1/2 cups milk
1 egg
1-1/2 cups self-rising flour
Salt and pepper
1/2 cup margarine

Double cube tenderloin or beat with a meat mallet for ideal texture; set aside.

Combine milk and egg, beating well; set aside. Combine flour, salt, and pepper in a bowl. Dredge tenderloin in flour mixture. Dip floured tenderloin in egg mixture, then dredge again in flour mixture.

Place margarine in a cast-iron skillet. Heat over medium-low until margarine melts. Add tenderloin to skillet and cook 6 to 8 minutes on each side or until golden brown. Yield: 6 servings

Sausage and Gravy

4 ounces uncooked sausage
2-1/2 tablespoons self-rising flour
1-1/2 cups milk
Salt and pepper to taste

Place sausage in a cast-iron skillet over medium-high heat, and cook, stirring to crumble, until sausage is done but not crispy brown. Add flour, salt, and pepper to skillet. Reduce heat to medium and cook, stirring constantly until browned. Stir in milk, and cook, stirring constantly, until smooth or gravy starts to boil. Yield: 4 servings

TRIMMINGS TO SERVE WITH
YOUR COUNTRY HAM

SIDES

Chick Peas in Olive Oil

1/4 cup olive oil
1 large yellow onion, finely chopped
2 large garlic cloves, minced
1-1/2-pound can chick peas, drained
Salt to taste
Freshly ground pepper to taste
2 teaspoons olive oil

Heat 1/4 cup olive oil over medium-high heat in a large skillet; add onion cook, stirring constantly, until tender. Add garlic and chickpeas; reduce heat to simmer and cook 10 minutes, adding a small amount of water, if necessary. Stir in salt. Transfer mixture to a serving bowl; grind pepper over top of chick peas and drizzle with remaining 2 tablespoons olive oil. Yield: 6 servings

Sliced Tomatoes with Melted Mozzarella

2 large ripe tomatoes, sliced 3/4-inch thick
Olive oil
About 1 cup shredded mozzarella cheese (may use sliced cheese)
Freshly grated black pepper

Place tomato slices on an ungreased baking sheet; brush with olive oil. Top tomato slices evenly with cheese. Bake at 400°F for 3 to 5 minutes or just until cheese melts. Grind black pepper over top of melted cheese, if desired. Yield: 6 servings

Glenda Johnson's Cheese Round

Sarah Brown uses Raggy O Peach Chutney, which is made locally in Smithfield, North Carolina

2 cups (8 ounces) grated sharp Cheddar cheese
4 ounces cream cheese, softened
1 clove garlic, minced
2 tablespoons sherry
4 to 5 tablespoons peach chutney
1/2 pound bacon, cooked and crumbled
3 green onions with tops, chopped

Combine Cheddar cheese and next 3 ingredients in a bowl, mixing well. Shape mixture into a round. Place cheese round on serving tray. Spread chutney on top of cheese round. Combine bacon and onions; cover top and sides of cheese round with bacon mixture. Serve with crackers. Yield: serves 6 to 8

Cheese Grits

1-1/2 cups water
1/2 teaspoon salt
1 tablespoon butter
1 cup uncooked regular grits
1/2 cup (2 ounces) shredded Cheddar cheese

In a quart saucepan, bring water, salt, and butter to a boil. Add grits, and return to boil. Remove from heat and stir in cheese. Yield: 10 (1/2-cup) servings

Fried Apple Rings

6 apples, washed, cored, and sliced into rings
2 tablespoons margarine
3 tablespoons water
3 tablespoons sugar

Heat margarine in heavy skillet. Add apples, and cook, uncovered, until apples are browned. Drain.

Place water in skillet; cover tightly and steam apples until tender. Sprinkle with sugar and serve hot. Yield: 12 servings

Fruit Shrub

Fill each 4- to 6-ounce appetizer glass with the following:
1/2 glass unsweetened orange juice
1/2 glass ginger ale
1 heaping spoonful lime sherbet

Serve immediately.

Corn Pudding

2 eggs
1/2 cup sugar
2 tablespoons all-purpose flour
1 teaspoon salt
Dash of pepper
1-1/2 cups milk
1 teaspoon vanilla extract (optional)
2 cups fresh or canned shoepeg corn kernels (if canned, drain)
2 tablespoons butter, melted
Paprika (optional)

Beat eggs in large bowl. Combine sugar, flour, salt, and pepper; add to eggs. Stir in milk and if desired, vanilla. Add corn and butter, stirring well. Pour mixture into a greased 8-inch square baking dish. Sprinkle with paprika, if desired. Bake at 350°F for 45 minutes to 1 hour, or until a knife inserted near the center comes out clean. Yield: 4 to 6 servings

Sweet Potato Casserole

This casserole can be prepared ahead and refrigerated or frozen before baking.

1/4 cup butter or margarine (1/2 stick)
3 cups cooked, mashed sweet potatoes (about 3 large)
1/2 cup sugar
2 eggs, beaten
1/3 cup milk
1 teaspoon vanilla extract

Topping:
1 cup brown sugar
1/2 cup all-purpose flour
2-1/2 tablespoons butter or margarine (about 1/3 stick), melted
1 cup chopped pecans

Combine first 6 ingredients in large bowl. Pour into a greased shallow 1-1/2 quart baking dish. Combine topping ingredients and crumble evenly over sweet potato mixture. Bake at 350°F for 25 minutes. Yield: 6 to 8 servings

Green Beans and Bacon

3/4 pound fresh green beans
8 slices Edwards' hickory-smoked bacon
2 medium-sized potatoes, peeled and cut into 1/2-inch pieces
1 small onion, sliced
1/4 cup water
1/2 teaspoon salt

Cook green beans in a small amount of boiling salted water for 10 to 15 minutes or until just tender; drain.

Chop bacon, place in a large, heavy skillet, and cook over medium heat until crisp. Add beans and remaining ingredients to skillet and cook, covered, 15 additional minutes or until potatoes are tender. Yield: 4 servings

Fried Apples

1 cup sugar
2 cups water
1/2 cup red cinnamon candies
4 medium cooking apples, peeled, cored, and sliced 1/2-inch thick

Combine sugar, water, and candies in a medium skillet. Cook over medium heat until sugar and candy melt. Add apple slices to skillet in a single layer. Simmer 3 to 4 minutes or just until tender; transfer cooked apples to a glass dish. Add remaining slices to skillet, adding water to cover apples, if necessary. Repeat until all apple slices are cooked. If necessary, continue to cook syrup remaining in skillet until slightly thickened; pour over apples. Allow apples and syrup to cool; cover and refrigerate. Yield: about 2 dozen slices

Sunshine Salad

1 (6-ounce) package orange gelatin
2 cups boiling water
1 cup grated carrots
1 (15-1/2-ounce) can crushed pineapple in heavy syrup, undrained

Combine gelatin and boiling water; cool slightly. Stir in carrots and pineapple. Pour mixture into a 13- x 9- 2-inch glass dish. Cover and refrigerate until set. Cut into squares to serve. Yield: 12 servings

Baked Turkey with Cornbread Dressing

1 (10- to 12-pound) turkey
1/4 cup butter, softened
1 onion
1 rib celery

Remove giblets and neck bones from turkey cavities. Rinse turkey and pat dry. Sprinkle cavity with salt and rub outside with softened butter. Place onion and celery inside cavity.

Arrange wing tips up and over back of turkey; tie turkey legs together with kitchen twine. Place turkey in roaster; cover and bake at 350°F for 20 minutes per pound (about 3 to 3-1/2 hours). After baking, discard onion and celery and reserve broth for dressing. Yield: 10 to 12 servings

Cornbread Dressing:

3 eggs
3 cups self-rising cornmeal
2 cups buttermilk
1/2 cup vegetable oil or bacon drippings
1/2 cup chopped celery
1/2 cup chopped onion
1 tablespoon sage
2 teaspoons pepper
2 to 3 cups turkey broth

Mix first four ingredients together; pour into a well-greased 12-inch cast iron skillet. Bake at 425°F for 20 minutes or until golden brown. Remove cornbread from skillet.

Crumble cornbread into a large bowl. Add celery, onion, sage, and pepper to crumbled cornbread. Stir in 2 or more cups of turkey broth or just enough to moisten. Pour into a well-greased 13- x 9- x 2-inch baking dish. Bake at 425°F for 35 to 40 minutes. Yield: 10 to 12 servings

Intoxicated Cranberry Relish

4 cups fresh cranberries
1 whole orange, quartered and seeds removed
1-3/4 cups sugar
3 tablespoons Jack Daniel's Whiskey

Using a food processor with the metal blade in place, place half the cranberries and half the orange into container; chop until coarsely ground. Transfer to a large bowl. Repeat with remaining cranberries and orange pieces. Combine cranberry mixture with sugar and Jack Daniel's Whiskey. Store in covered container in refrigerator overnight for flavors to ripen. Yield: 3-1/2 cups

Macaroni and Cheese

8 cups water
2 teaspoons salt
1/4 cup vegetable oil
2 cups uncooked macaroni
2 cups cubed American process cheese (Velveeta)
1/4 cup butter
1/2 cup shredded sharp Cheddar cheese

In a large saucepan bring water and salt to a boil. Add oil and macaroni, stirring occasionally. Cook until tender; drain. Add process cheese and butter, stirring well. Pour mixture into a buttered 13- x 9- x -2-inch baking dish. Top evenly with Cheddar cheese. Bake at 350°F for 20 minutes or until hot and bubbly. Yield: 6 to 8 servings

Tipsy Sweet Potatoes

2-1/2 cups cooked, mashed sweet potatoes
1/4 cup butter, softened
1/2 cup firmly packed light brown sugar
Pinch of salt
1/3 cup Jack Daniel's Whiskey
Pecan halves or marshmallows for topping

Combine all ingredients except pecans or marshmallows. Spoon into a greased 1-quart baking dish. Top with pecan halves or marshmallows. Bake at 325°F for 20 to 25 minutes or until bubbly. Yield: 6 to 8 servings

Fried Okra

1 (10-ounce) box frozen sliced okra, or 1-1/2 cups sliced fresh okra
Salt and pepper to taste
About 1/2 cup cornmeal, preferably white
Lard or vegetable oil

Let frozen okra drain in a colander for 30 minutes (fresh okra does not need to be drained). Season with salt and pepper. Place okra in a bowl and add enough cornmeal to coat each slice.

Place 1/2 inch of lard or vegetable oil in a cast iron or other heavy skillet and place over medium-high heat. When oil is hot, add okra one layer deep. Cook 5 minutes, until browned on one side, then turn okra and cook on other side. Remove okra with a slotted spoon and drain on paper towels. When all okra has been cooked, heat briefly in a hot oven; serve immediately. Yield: 4 to 6 servings

BREADS

Bruschetta

6 (1-1/2-inch thick) slices Italian bread
2 large garlic cloves, peeled and cut in half
2 tablespoons olive oil

Place bread slices on a baking sheet. Bake at 400°F for 5 minutes or until toasted. Rub top of toasted bread with garlic; drizzle bread slices evenly with olive oil. Yield: 6 servings

Hot Rolls

1 package dry yeast
1/2 cup lukewarm water
1/2 cup lard or shortening
1/2 cup boiling water
1/4 cup sugar
1 teaspoon salt
1 egg, beaten
About 3-1/2 cups all-purpose flour

Combine yeast and 1/2 cup lukewarm water; stir to dissolve yeast. Set aside.

Place lard in a large mixing bowl. Pour boiling water over lard. Stir in sugar, salt, egg, and yeast mixture. Add flour gradually, beating it in well.

When dough is stiff, turn it out onto a floured surface and knead until smooth, elastic, and no longer sticky, adding more flour, if necessary. Pull off pieces of dough large enough to shape into 2-1/2-inch balls. Place the balls side by side, nearly touching in a greased 9-inch square pan.

Cover dough with plastic wrap and let sit in a warm, draft-free place about 1 hour or until rolls have doubled in size. Bake at 425°F for 25 minutes or until golden brown. Yield: about 1 dozen rolls

Buttermilk Biscuits

2-1/2 cups all-purpose flour
1/4 teaspoon baking soda
1/2 teaspoon salt
2-1/2 tablespoons baking powder
3/4 cup shortening
1-1/2 cups buttermilk

Sift together flour, baking soda, salt, and baking powder, Cut shortening into flour mixture. Add buttermilk gradually, stirring until mixture is well moistened.

Turn dough out onto a floured surface and knead 4 or 5 times. Roll dough out to 1/2-inch thickness. Cut with a 3-inch round cutter and place on a greased baking sheet. Bake at 425°F for 10 to 12 minutes. Yield: 2 dozen biscuits

Refrigerator Rolls

The "secret" ingredient in this recipe is cooked, mashed potatoes. Just be sure to save the water in which the potatoes are cooked---it goes in the dough! The best part is that the dough can be made ahead of time and stored in the refrigerator for about a week.

2 packages dry yeast
1 cup lukewarm water
2 cups cooked, mashed potatoes
1-1/3 cups shortening
1-1/2 cups sugar
1 tablespoon salt
2 cups potato water
3 eggs, beaten
About 18 cups all-purpose flour

Dissolve yeast in lukewarm water. Using an electric mixer combine mashed potatoes, shortening, sugar, and salt in a large bowl. Add potato water; allow mixture to cool. Add yeast mixture and eggs, beating well to mix. Stir in enough flour to mixture to make a stiff dough. (Dough will be sticky.)

Turn dough out onto a floured surface and knead 2 to 5 minutes. Place dough in a greased bowl, turning to grease top of dough. Cover tightly and refrigerate until ready to use.

Shape dough into 2-inch balls and place on greased baking sheets or in greased muffin pans. Cover lightly and place in a warm place about 1 hour or until doubled in bulk. Brush tops of rolls with melted shortening and bake at 400°F for 20 minutes. Yield: about 4 dozen rolls

Silver Dollar Pancakes

1-3/4 cups all-purpose flour
2 tablespoons sugar
2 tablespoons baking powder
1 teaspoon salt
2 eggs, beaten
1/2 cup vegetable oil
1-1/2 cups milk

Sift together flour, sugar, baking powder, and salt in a large bowl; set aside. Combine eggs, oil, and milk; add to flour mixture, stirring until well blended.

Spoon small amounts of batter onto greased hot griddle to make 2-inch pancakes. Cook until edges bubble, then turn pancakes and cook until golden brown. Yield: about 2 dozen pancakes

Blueberry Muffins

Recipe may be halved, or baked muffins may be frozen.

4 eggs, beaten
2 cups sugar
1 cup vegetable oil
1 teaspoon vanilla extract
4 cups all-purpose flour
1 teaspoon salt
1 teaspoon baking soda
1 teaspoon baking powder
2 cups (16 ounces) sour cream
2 cups blueberries (or 2 cups chopped strawberries or cored, chopped apples)

Beat eggs. Gradually add sugar. Gradually add oil; stir in vanilla. Combine flour, salt, baking soda, and baking powder; add alternately to egg mixture with sour cream. Fold in blueberries. Spoon into greased muffin pans, filling half full. Bake at 350°F for 10 to 12 minutes. Yield: 3 dozen muffins

Cinnamon Rolls

Basic Sweet Dough is used at The Dillard House for making these rolls that are a must on every breakfast menu.

1 recipe Basic Sweet Dough (Page 147)
1/4 cup butter, melted
1/2 cup light brown sugar
1 teaspoon ground cinnamon
Glaze

Divide dough in half; set one half aside. Knead dough on a lightly floured surface until smooth, elastic, and no longer sticky. Roll out to a 1/4-inch thick rectangle. Spread with half of melted butter and sprinkle with half of brown sugar. Sprinkle half of cinnamon over brown sugar.

Roll up dough jelly-roll style and cut into 1/2-inch slices. Repeat with remaining half of dough and ingredients.

Place slices on a greased baking sheet 1/2-inch apart. Set in a warm place and let rise until doubled in size. Bake at 350°F for 10 to 12 minutes. Drizzle with Glaze while warm. Yield: 2 dozen cinnamon rolls

Glaze:

1-1/2 cups confectioner's sugar
3 tablespoons hot water
2 teaspoons butter, softened
1 teaspoon vanilla extract

Mix all ingredients, stirring until smooth and creamy. Spread on warm cinnamon rolls. Yield: enough for 2 dozen cinnamon rolls

Basic Sweet Dough

3/4 cup milk
1/4 cup sugar
1/4 cup lukewarm water
1/4 cup butter, softened
1 package active dry yeast
1 egg, beaten
3-1/4 to 3-1/2 cups self-rising flour

Scald milk; stir in sugar and butter, and let cool to lukewarm; set aside.

Measure lukewarm water into a large, warm mixing bowl. Sprinkle yeast over water and stir until yeast dissolves. Add milk mixture to yeast mixture. Stir in egg, and half the flour; mix until smooth. Stir in enough of remaining flour to make a soft dough.

For lightness, add only enough flour to make a dough you can handle. Cover, and refrigerate 8 hours or overnight. Dough may be stored in refrigerator for 3 to 4 days. Yield: enough for 2 dozen cinnamon rolls

SWEET THINGS

Jack Daniel's Brownies and Glaze

3/4 cup all-purpose flour
1/2 teaspoon baking powder
1/2 teaspoon salt
1/4 cup plus 2 tablespoons butter
3 ounces baking chocolate
3/4 cup sugar
2 eggs
1 cup chopped pecans or walnuts
1 teaspoon vanilla extract
2 ounces Jack Daniel's Whiskey

Mix together flour, baking powder and salt; set aside. Melt butter and chocolate in top of double boiler over simmering water. Remove from heat; add sugar, eggs, nuts, vanilla, and flour mixture. Stir in Jack Daniel's Whiskey; mix well.

Pour batter into a greased 9-inch square baking pan. Bake at 350°F for 25 minutes. Remove from oven and top with glaze. Yield: 16 brownies

Jack Daniel's Brownie Glaze

1 cup confectioner's sugar
1-1/2 teaspoons boiling water
1 tablespoon plus 1 teaspoon Jack Daniel's Whiskey
1/8 teaspoon vanilla extract

Combine all ingredients; stir until smooth. Brush on or pour over brownies.

Grandmother Jester's Applesauce Cake (1918)
We like to use applesauce made with Granny Smith apples for this cake. Lard seems to be the key to the outstanding flavor of this moist cake, but you can substitute shortening.

2 cups warm applesauce
2 teaspoons baking soda
1 (15-ounce) box raisins
4 cups all-purpose flour
1 teaspoon ground cinnamon
1 teaspoon nutmeg
1/2 cup lard or shortening
2 cups sugar
1 cup chopped pecans

Combine applesauce and baking soda; set aside. Dredge raisins in small amount of flour; set aside. Add cinnamon and nutmeg to remaining flour; set aside.

Place lard in a large bowl. Beat with an electric mixer until fluffy. Gradually add sugar, beating well after each addition. Add applesauce mixture to creamed mixture alternately with flour mixture. Stir in raisins and pecans.

Spoon batter into a greased and floured 10-inch tube pan. Bake at 325°F for 1 hour or until cake tests done. Shield top of cake with foil during last 30 minutes of baking to prevent excess browning, if necessary. Yield: one 10-inch cake

Appendix A

TROUBLESHOOTING: HOME-CURING PROBLEMS TO AVOID

The two most common mistakes amateur ham curers make are applying the cure when the weather is too warm, then not refrigerating the ham; and not properly protecting aging hams from insects. In the early days, hams were coated with black pepper because of the natural tendency of pepper to repel insects. Storing hams tied tightly in brown bags or cloth sacks that are free of rips also helps make it difficult for insects to reach them.

Nancy Newsom, of Col. Newsom's Aged Hams in Princeton, Kentucky, uses the same weather-dependent curing process as home-curers. "The biggest problem for us is too much damp mold during spring months when it rains a lot," she says.

To counteract the mold problem Nancy keeps extra ventilation and fans going in the aging room. "Just keep some air moving over the surface of the hams to keep the mold down," she advises.

Listed below are other typical problems encountered by home curers and what to do about them:

Ham isn't uniform in size or shape.

Be sure to select hams for curing or live hogs from a specific weight range. Live hogs weighing from

225 to 265 pounds will produce hams that weigh 16 to 22 pounds.

To make sure that the hams are of uniform shape, they should be separated from the pork carcass by cutting through the center of the hock. The ham and loin should be separated between the second and third sacral vertebrae (second vertebra from the juncture of the rump and back) and cut perpendicular to the long axis of the shank.

Growth of bacteria on pork

Make sure hogs used for meat are free of abscesses and bruises. Processing should be handled in clean facilities. Equipment and facilities should be cleaned with procedures proven to reduce contamination of pork during processing.

Even in sanitary conditions, bacterial growth can occur. To reduce this possibility to the minimum, store pork as close to 32°F as possible prior to curing. Certain bacteria grow about ten times faster at 38°F than at 32°F.

Also, make sure that fresh pork is chilled properly after slaughter; this will reduce moisture loss and improve the color and firmness of the meat.

Pale, soft pork that weeps moisture

This condition is called PSE--pale, soft, exudative pork. This problem causes pale colored ham that has a gray or green tinge after curing. The weeping meat causes additional weight loss during curing and makes the ham more difficult to handle because of the moisture.

The soft muscle structure causes more muscle separation and uneven cure penetration. When muscles separate, there is a greater chance of microbial contamination and insect invasion during storage.

Choose hogs that have 0.6 inch or more of average backfat thickness over the shoulder and neck. Do not use hogs with evidence of porcine stress syndrome for curing or as replacement stock.

Negative results of a PSE ham can be minimized by keeping the pork at the proper temperature from the time it is harvested through curing.

Uneven salt equalization and penetration of cure

Pork cured when the humidity is too high will not equalize properly, which leaves the meat with too much moisture when the cure process is complete. Dry-cured meat should lose at least 18% moisture; most curers strive for at least 20% loss.

If the relative humidity is above 80%, you can use a fan, furnace, or other means of forced air movement to help the ham to lose more moisture.

Color doesn't develop properly

Incomplete color development can be caused by using too much nitrite or nitrate in the cure mixture. Various microorganisms also can impair the color development. If microorganisms are the cause, the ham will also sour and begin rotting.

Color fades during storage

Ham color fades through an insufficient amount aging or if oxidation occurs under ultraviolet radiation or in the presence of oxygen. Most lighting contains some ultraviolet rays, so hams should be stored in cool, dark places. Restrict the presence of oxygen exposure to the ham by vacuum packaging or using other wrappings that oxygen cannot penetrate. Smoking does help fix the cured color somewhat.

Aged flavor doesn't develop

Age home cured pork cuts at least 3 months and up to 1 year or longer.

Pork tastes rancid

Cured pork develops a ripe, rancid taste as a result of the salt cure process. For a milder cured ham flavor, use a shorter aging period, and do not freeze the ham. Storing cured meat in the freezer for long periods of time can increase the strong flavor.

Cured ham has a stronger rancid flavor when it isn't stored properly. If you freeze it, use the best grade of freezer wrapping paper and use the drugstore wrap method. Remove as much air from the packaging as possible before storage. Store frozen country ham at -10°F or colder.

Meat sours, becomes tainted, or putrefies

Souring and putrefication of meat is caused by bacterial contamination that usually occurs before the curing process. It can occur if the fresh ham is stored too long (over 5 days) or at a temperature that is too high (over 35°F).

Contamination also can occur if conditions in the cure area, smokehouse, or aging area are unsanitary, or if the cure ingredients are contaminated.

Tainting is caused by pork that has a higher pH (level of acidity) than normal. It is harder for the cure to penetrate the muscle tissue. In addition, the higher pH stimulates bacterial growth. This condition is less common if the cure process is started sooner after slaughter.

Mold growth

Mold growth is common among cured, aged meat. You can lessen the growth by storing cured meat in a dry, well-ventilated room with a temperature of 45 to 55°F and a relative humidity of less than 68%. Unwrapped meat should not touch other meat. Storing cured meat this way increases moisture loss, but it's less expensive than meat loss from trimming mold.

Insect infestation

Cured meats are commonly attacked by cheese skippers, larder beetles, red-legged ham beetles, and mites.

1. Cheese skipper: This insect gets its name from the jumping habit of the larvae that bore through cheese and cured meat. Meat infested with skippers quickly rots and becomes slimy. An adult fly is two-winged and one-third the size of a housefly. It lays eggs on meat and cheese and multiplies rapidly.

2. Larder beetle: The adult larder beetle is about 1/3-inch long and dark brown with a yellow band across its back. The fuzzy, brownish larva feed on or just beneath the cured meat surface, but do not rot the meat.

3. Red-legged ham beetle: The purplish larvae are about 1/3-inch long and bore through meat, causing it to dry rot. The adult is about 1/4-inch long, brilliant greenish blue with red legs and is red at the base of the antennae. This beetle feeds on the meat surface.

4. Mites: Mites are whitish in color and about 1/32-inch long at maturity. Parts of meat affected with mites become powdery.

The first step of insect prevention is to slaughter hogs during cold weather when the insects are inactive. Install screens or double entryways in smoking or aging areas to prevent flies, ants, and other insects that carry mites from entering.

Skippers feed and breed on grease and tiny scraps of meat lodged in cracks, so keep aging and storage areas properly cleaned. To prevent meat from lodging between board cracks, seal the cracks with putty or plastic wood after cleaning.

After cleaning and sealing the cracks, spray a thin layer of insecticide on the floor to kill crawling insects. Spray the aging area once every three months with a pyrethrin spray. Synergized pyrethrins, such as piperonyl butoxide, may be applied with a paint brush if the room is stocked with meat. If you must spray, remove the meat from the room before spraying. Spray the floor, walls, and other surfaces where houseflies and other pests may crawl or land. All spray should be thoroughly dried before returning meat to the room.

BE SURE TO FOLLOW ALL MIXING AND APPLICATION DIRECTIONS ON THE PESTICIDE LABEL.

If hams become infested after all of the above precautions have been taken, remove the ham from storage and trim away the infested area of the ham. Be sure to trim deep enough to remove larvae that have penetrated along the bone and through the fat.

To protect the newly exposed lean areas, cover the cut surface with vegetable oil or melted shortening to delay molding or drying. It's safe to eat the uninfested portion, but you should cook it right away.

The Authors

Norman G. Marriott, Ph.D., is Professor emeritus in Food Science at Virginia Polytechnic Institute and State University , in Blacksburg, Virginia. He has long had a personal interest in country ham, both as a researcher and a partaker of this treat. Dr. Marriott has judged many cured meat shows in the United States and spoken in many countries about country ham.

Herbert W. Ockerman, Ph.D., is a Professor in Animal Science at Ohio State University. He travels around the world lecturing about meat science, and is well recognized for his international contributions.

ORDER FORM

The Ultimate Guide to Country Ham
An American Delicacy

Name : _____

Shipping Address:_____

_____

Phone: _____   e-mail:_____

No. Of Copies ____ @ $16.00 =   Total $_____

Plus Shipping: _____@ $3.00 per book $_____

TOTAL DUE: $_____

Make checks payable to **Norman G. Marriott**

Send order form to:
N.G. Marriott
180 Diamond Ave.
Christiansburg, VA 24073
Phone: 540-382-8206
E-mail: marriott@vt.edu